THE SPIRIT OF TIBETAN BUDDHISM

THE SPIRIT OF TIBETAN BUDDHISM

SAM VAN SCHAIK

PUBLISHED IN ASSOCIATION WITH
THE INTERNATIONAL SACRED LITERATURE TRUST

YALE UNIVERSITY PRESS
NEW HAVEN AND LONDON

For information about this and other Yale University Press publications please contact:
U.S. Office: sales.press@yale.edu   yalebooks.com
Europe Office: sales@yaleup.co.uk   yalebooks.co.uk

Typeset in Arno by IDSUK (DataConnection) Ltd
Printed in Great Britain by TJ International Ltd, Padstow, Cornwall

Library of Congress Cataloging-in-Publication Data

Names: Van Schaik, Sam, author.
Title: The spirit of Tibetan Buddhism / Sam van Schaik.
Description: New Haven : Yale University Press, 2016.
LCCN 2015042853 | ISBN 9780300198751 (cl : alk. paper)
LCSH: Buddhism–Tibet Region.
Classification: LCC BQ7604 .V36 2016 | DDC 294.3/923–dc23
LC record available at http://lccn.loc.gov/2015042853

A catalogue record for this book is available from the British Library.

10 9 8 7 6 5 4 3 2 1

MIX
Paper from responsible sources
FSC® C013056
FSC www.fsc.org

To Lama Jampa Thaye

CONTENTS

CHAPTER ONE

AN INTRODUCTION TO THE PRACTICE OF TIBETAN BUDDHISM

'Tibetan Buddhism' is a name for all the Buddhist texts and practices that have come from Tibet and are now practised not just in Tibet but also across the world. In fact, Tibetan Buddhism has been an international religion for centuries, flourishing in China, Mongolia, Bhutan, and Nepal as well as Tibet. More recently Tibetan Buddhism has gained global popularity and is being taught not only by teachers from these Asian countries, but also by those from Europe, the Americas, and elsewhere. As Tibetan Buddhism grows and changes, in time the name 'Tibetan Buddhism' may become redundant, but it still makes sense for now, as these practices remain closely linked to their Tibetan heritage.[1]

Practitioners of Tibetan Buddhism include both monastics (monks and nuns) and lay people. The Tibetan tradition accords as much respect to accomplished lay teachers and meditators as it does to ordained ones, so the two types of practitioner form no sort of hierarchy. In general, monks and nuns live in monasteries and follow the Buddhist monastic vows, which, among other things, commit them to celibacy. Their day-to-day life is largely determined by the schedule of the monastery, which usually involves several daily recitation practices.

Lay practitioners, who often have jobs and families, express their commitment in different ways, such as regular meditation practice at home, group practices at a Tibetan Buddhist temple or centre, studying Buddhist texts, and other meritorious activities. Whereas in Asian cultures lay Buddhists tend to have been brought up with the religion, in Western cultures they are more likely to be converts, although some Asian countries, such as China, Taiwan, and Nepal, are increasingly seeing converts to Tibetan Buddhism.

Those who make a commitment to Tibetan Buddhism usually have a teacher, and that teacher will belong to one or more of the main schools of Tibetan Buddhism: Nyingma, Sakya, Kagyu, and Gelug. Each school has its own lineages of teachings, passed down through the centuries, and a teacher's affiliation with a particular school will determine the nature of their students' meditation practice and the texts that they study. The relationship between teacher and student is taken very seriously and is often compared to that between a patient and a doctor, with the Buddha's teachings, or *dharma*, being the medicine.[2]

In a wider circle around the teacher and his or her lay students is the Buddhist community or *sangha*. In its broadest and most inclusive sense, the *sangha* includes all Buddhists, all over the world. But the word is more often used to refer to smaller communities, the monks and lay people associated with a particular monastery, teacher, or Buddhist centre. It is these groups that will come together for the regular practices of listening to teachings, meditation, recitation of prayers, and other ritual activities. Thus Tibetan Buddhism is far from the inward-looking, self-involved practice that images of meditating monks might suggest.

What, then, is Tibetan Buddhism for? Or, to put it another way, what is the attraction for those who were not born into this tradition? Like all other Buddhist traditions, Tibetan Buddhism is informed by the original motivation expressed by the Buddha in his early sermons: to escape the cycle of suffering by losing one's illusions and 'waking up' (Sanskrit, *budh*) to the way things really are. The will to become an awakened person (Skt. *buddha*) is motivated by love and compassion, and the wish to free all sentient beings from suffering.

As in other Buddhist traditions, investigation into the nature of the mind and reality plays an important part in Tibetan Buddhism. In fact it is probably the most philosophically sophisticated modern Buddhist tradition, not only having preserved the major philosophical schools that developed in India, but also with a vibrant tradition of philosophical thought, commentary, and debate. Sometimes it is asked whether Buddhism should be considered a religion or a philosophy. That question is based on a distinction between religion and philosophy that arose in seventeenth-century Europe; in Buddhism it makes little sense to try to tease them apart. Philosophy is present in Buddhism, but always in the service of liberation from suffering. Thus, despite certain similarities, comparisons between Buddhist philosophies and modern academic philosophy are likely to be unsatisfactory because of their quite different aims.

What makes Tibetan Buddhism different from other Buddhist traditions, such as the Theravada, or the Zen schools of Japan, is the great variety of practices that were brought to Tibet from India and incorporated into the Buddhist path. These practices comprise the three 'vehicles' (so called because each represents a way of travelling the path to enlightenment): the early teachings of the Buddha, known in Tibet as the vehicle of the hearers, or the lesser vehicle (*hīnayāna*); the scriptures and practices of the greater vehicle (*mahāyāna*); and the full range of practices of the diamond vehicle (*vajrayāna*). Since the practices of *vajrayāna* derive from texts known as tantras, *vajrayāna* is also commonly known as 'tantric Buddhism'.

A little more should be said about these three vehicles. The *hīnayāna* refers to teachings that are now practised by the Theravada sect in South and Southeast Asia, but since members of the Theravada certainly do not consider their path to be 'lesser', they do not accept it as a description. Thus the term *hīnayāna* is only used by those who consider themselves as belonging to the *mahāyāna,* as a way of distinguishing the scriptures (*sūtra*) and practices that are specific to their 'greater' vehicle. The main differentiating feature of the *mahāyāna* is the importance of the ideal of the bodhisattva, who strives for liberation not only for him or herself, but for all living beings, and the practices associated with bodhisattvas such as Tārā, the embodiment of compassionate activity.[3]

For most people it is the artwork, material culture, and ritual practices of the *vajrayāna* that give Tibetan Buddhism its distinct character. Yet the *vajrayāna* is considered to be an extension of the *mahāyāna,* not a departure, as the *vajrayāna* is still based on the motivation to save all sentient beings from the cycle of suffering, but with more powerful practices to accomplish this aim. Thus there is no great disconnect from other Buddhist traditions. The great success of the practitioners and scholars of Tibet was to integrate the tantric practices of the *vajrayāna* with the aims and philosophy of *mahāyāna* in coherent systems of practice (or 'paths'), starting at the beginning of spiritual practice and ending with the state of enlightenment itself. This idea of an integrated practice is expressed by this verse from a nineteenth-century teacher's letter to his students:

> From the difficulty of obtaining leisure and endowment,
> Through to the development and perfection stages of secret
> mantra,
> And the direct path of *dzogchen,* the practice of cutting through,
> There is no teaching not included here.[4]

In the chapters of this book I hope to give a sense of this rich variety in Tibetan Buddhism and the way the spiritual path is set out in a clear and coherent fashion. It is the nature of this progress that nothing is left behind. Each stage includes the last, but adds more subtlety and depth. In the end, the state of enlightenment includes everything that came before, and is found always to have been there from the beginning.[5]

Buddhism in Tibet

Tibetan Buddhists have been historians of their religion since at least the tenth century. A millennium of historical writing has therefore resulted in an extremely rich tradition of history from which to draw. For Tibetan Buddhists, the writing and reading of religious histories is also a form of practice; an approach quite different from the Western post-Enlightenment idea of what history should be. The Tibetan historians did believe that a historical account should be true, but equally important to them was the role of history in religious practice.

Every teacher and every practice is part of a lineage, and histories of Tibetan Buddhism are above all histories of lineages. It is said that one should begin by examining a teacher, then develop an attitude of devotion towards them and their lineage, and finally begin to emulate their realization and activities.[6]

It is because of the importance of the teacher–student relationship that the Tibetan Buddhist tradition emphasizes the importance of assessing prospective teachers before asking to be taught by them. Part of this process is assessing whether the practices that the teacher is offering have a genuine provenance. This is one of the functions of reading religious histories. Once a student has identified a teacher and received teachings from him or her, putting those teachings into practice consistently requires an attitude of devotion (in modern terms, we might instead say respect and commitment). This too is a function of reading histories, which are written to support a student's respectful attitude towards teachers from his or her own practice lineage, and towards his or her own teacher as their representative.

Traditional Tibetan histories of Buddhism always begin with the Buddha Śākyamuni and the beginnings of Buddhism in India. Śākyamuni taught during the fifth or fourth centuries BCE; after his death his teachings, or *dharma*, were gathered into collections of *sūtras*, which were transmitted orally. Later, the rules for Buddhist monks were collected and standardized in the *vinaya*. Around the second and first centuries BCE, philosophical elaborations of the Buddha's teachings, known as *abhidharma*, began to be written down. These are the 'three baskets' (*tripiṭaka*) of the Buddha's teaching accepted by all schools of Buddhism.

During these centuries, Buddhism spread throughout India, thanks in part to the patronage of the emperor Aśoka (304–232 BCE). In the first centuries of the new millennium, Buddhism began to spread even further afield, to Central Asia, China and Southeast Asia. The *sūtras* of the *mahāyāna* began to circulate, and new commentaries and treatises (*śāstra*) were written. From around the sixth century CE onward, the new practices of the *vajrayāna* began to be circulated in texts known as *tantras*. Thus, by the time Buddhism arrived in Tibet in the seventh century, it had been through more than a thousand years of development in India.

Traditional accounts of Buddhism in Tibet begin with the reign of the emperor Songtsen Gampo, in the first half of the seventh century. Songtsen Gampo, whose empire stretched from northern India and Nepal to the kingdoms of the Silk Road, is said to have married two foreign princesses, one from Nepal and the other from China. Both princesses brought statues of the Buddha from their homelands, and Songtsen Gampo built temples to house the statues. The Tibetan tradition considers the beginning of Buddhism in Tibet to be the bringing of these Buddhist art objects into the country and the architectural response to their presence.

Modern historians cast doubt on aspects of this story; for example, the Nepalese princess may or may not have existed. But there is little doubt that the Jokhang temple, which still stands in Lhasa, was built during the reign of Songtsen Gampo, with the help of Nepalese architects and craftsmen. It was not until a century later, in the reign of Tri Song Detsen (r.756–c.800) that Buddhism was adopted as the state religion of Tibet. Thanks to the efforts of the emperor and his court, a great translation bureau was established to translate the *tripiṭaka* and the *śāstras* into Tibetan. A major monastery was built in Samye, and the first Tibetan monks were ordained. Two foreign teachers were of great importance in this effort: the scholarly abbot Śāntarakṣita, and the *vajrayāna* master Padmasambhava. While Śāntarakṣita was important in the transmission of scholastic Buddhism to Tibet, Padmasambhava became a kind of cult hero, seen as a second Buddha.

Despite the gradual collapse of the Tibetan empire in the second half of the ninth century, Buddhism continued to gain popularity in Tibet, especially the tantric practices of *vajrayāna* Buddhism. Beginning in the late tenth century, the popularity of the *vajrayāna* led Tibetans to travel to India in search of new teachings and practices. Some of these Tibetan teachers and translators gained large followings and were able to establish their own monasteries. Gradually these monasteries became the new centres of power, both religious and political. This became known as 'the second diffusion of Buddhism' in Tibet, while those who remained faithful to the lineages from the imperial period, 'the first diffusion', came to be called the *Nyingma* ('old ones').[7]

The schools of Tibetan Buddhism

Nyingma

The Nyingma were never really a school as such, although since the re-configuring of Tibetan Buddhism outside of Tibet, they are now more like a school, with a recognizable identity and a head lama. In the past, the name Nyingma referred to teachers who traced their lineages back through the first diffusion of Buddhism in Tibet during the time of the empire. The greater part of the *tripiṭaka* was translated into Tibetan during this time and is shared by all of the schools, so it is only in the tantric texts and practices that the old and new schools differ from each other. The Nyingma tantric tradition includes texts that have been transmitted from the time of the empire, known as *kama* (Tibetan, *bka' ma*) or 'Buddha's word', and revealed texts known as *terma* (*gter ma*) or 'hidden treasures'.

From the eleventh century through to the present day, treasure revealers or *terton* (*gter ston*) have revealed these new teachings, discovered in physical hiding places or in visionary experiences. Most of these are attributed to Padmasambhava. After concealing a treasure teaching, Padmasambhava is said to have given one of his disciples a blessing and a prophecy that the disciple would be the one to discover it in a future life. The teachings revealed by these *terton* are thought to be particularly effective for the time in which they were discovered, and although the *terma* are generally from the Nyingma school, other schools have accepted some of them as well.[8]

The tantric texts and practices of the Nyingma are not especially different from those of the new schools. The exception is *dzogchen*, 'the great perfection', a complex of practices that are only found in the

Nyingma school. In *dzogchen* it is said that there is no difference between an enlightened buddha and an ordinary person; the nature of mind is pure from the start (*ka dag*). The basic method of *dzogchen* is an introduction to this enlightened state of awareness (*rig pa*) given by a master to a student. This introduction does not invalidate further practice, but provides the basic view of reality that informs that practice. The *dzogchen* teachings, most of which have appeared as *terma,* were systematized by Longchenpa (1308–63) and are commonly practised in the present day through the texts of Jigme Lingpa (1730–98).[9]

Kadam

The Kadam school was established by disciples of the Indian master Atiśa (see chapter three) in the eleventh century. Beginning at the monastery of Radreng in central Tibet, the Kadampas quickly spread throughout Tibet, even reaching the Tangut kingdom in Central Asia in the twelfth century. The Kadampas were exclusively monastic and had a strong scholarly bent. They are also known for their development of the 'mind-training' genre of practices (see chapter four). The Kadampas also popularized the idea of a graduated path (*lam rim*) incorporating the teachings of the *hīnayāna, mahāyāna,* and *vajrayāna*. The Kadampas began to decline by the middle of the fourteenth century and soon disappeared as an independent school. Yet Kadam teachings and lineages remained hugely influential in Tibetan Buddhism.[10]

Sakya

The Sakya school began with the founding of a temple in the region of Sakya by Khon Konchog Gyalpo (1034–1120). Attracted to the new tantric lineages being taught in Tibet, such as those of the *Hevajra Tantra,* Konchog Gyalpo studied with the translator Drogmi Lotsawa, while maintaining some of the older teachings as well. He passed on his lineage to his son, Kunga Nyingpo, known as Sachen, 'the great Sakyapa'. Sachen specialized in the practices of the *lamdre,* meaning 'the path that includes the result', an advanced system of meditation based on the *Hevajra Tantra.*

Sachen passed the lineage to his two sons, Dragpa Gyaltsen and Sonam Tsemo (the author of the text translated in chapter six). The Khon family has remained at the head of the Sakya school to the present day, and this family lineage means that the head of the Sakya school has generally not been a monk. After Dragpa Gyaltsen and Sonam Tsemo, the next head of the school, Sakya Paṇḍita (1182–1251) was renowned throughout Tibet for his scholarship. He was invited to the court of the Mongol emperor in 1244, as a representative of the religious and secular leaders of Tibet, and remained there until his death. His nephew, Chogyal Pagpa (1235–80), became a favourite of Kubilai Khan, who granted him suzerainty over all Tibet in exchange for a *vajrayāna* initiation.

After this heyday, the political fortunes of the Sakya school declined somewhat, though two new branches of the school appeared in the fifteenth century: the Ngor school, based at the monastery of that name; and the Tshar school, based at Nalendra monastery. The Sakya school continued to be known for expertise in both tantric practice and scholasticism, with teachers such as Gorampa Sonam Senge (1429–89; see chapters four and five) embodying both of these aspects of practice.[11]

Kagyu

This name actually describes a whole group of lineages, of which all but one trace back to the translator Marpa Lotsawa (1012–97). Marpa travelled to India three times, where he received tantric teachings from the Indian masters Naropa and Maitripa. From the former he received the advanced tantric practices of the 'six yogas of Naropa'; from the latter he received the instructions of *mahāmudrā*, 'the great seal', on resting in the natural state of mind, from which realization arises. *Mahāmudrā* is similar to the *dzogchen* of the Nyingma school, and the two have been combined by some Kagyu and Nyingma teachers.

Although Marpa intended to pass on his lineage to his sons, it was his famous disciple Milarepa, a hermit who had previously committed murder with black magic, who carried on the teachings of Naropa and

Maitripa, and passed them on to a Kadampa monk called Gampopa. The latter brought monasticism and Kadam scholasticism to the Kagyu, though it remained primarily a meditation-oriented tradition. After Gampopa, the Kagyu lineage split into schools founded by his disciples: (i) the Phagmodru Kagyu, which later split into eight further schools; (ii) the Barom Kagyu; (iii) the Tsalpa Kagyu; and (iv) the Karma Kagyu. The last of these is the most widespread of the Kagyu schools, headed by the reborn lamas known as the Karmapas. Among the schools that split from the Phagmodru Kagyu, the Drugpa Kagyu became the state school of Bhutan.[12]

Gelug

This school, also known as Ganden, after its first major monastery, is based on the teachings of Tsongkhapa Lozang Dragpa (1376–1419). It was the last of the major schools to be founded in Tibet and differs from the others in that it is not based on lineages brought from India. Instead, the Gelug adopted most of their tantric practices from the Sakya school. Tsongkhapa also studied philosophy in the Sakya curriculum, which dominated Tibetan scholasticism at the time, and later developed his own interpretations.

Tsongkhapa developed a form of the graduated path that incorporated the mind-training of the Kadampas with tantric practices from Sakya lineages, all informed by his own philosophical writings. The most distinct aspect of Tsongkhapa's teaching was this philosophy; it is perhaps for this reason that later Gelug scholars have tended to hold to a consistent philosophical position based on Tsongkhapa's works, rather than the pluralism observable in most other Tibetan schools.

Tsongkhapa and his students were monks, and, unlike the other Tibetan Buddhist schools, the Gelug has been exclusively monastic and has built Tibet's largest and most populous monasteries. In the seventeenth century the fifth Dalai Lama established Gelug rule over central and western Tibet with the military backing of the Mongols and later the Manchus. Afterwards, the Gelug school dominated Tibetan Buddhism throughout Tibet (apart from in the eastern regions of Kham and Amdo), and the Dalai Lamas were, at least in theory, the supreme rulers of Tibet.[13]

Reading the texts

This book is an introduction to the path of Tibetan Buddhism. I have based each chapter on a significant text that is still read and put into practice, and although my translations of these texts can only offer glimpses of the manifold world of Tibetan Buddhism, I believe they will give a better sense of it than an attempt to simplify and synthesize could achieve.

I have set the chapters out in a rough approximation of the path itself, beginning with the basic ethical code shared by all Buddhists (chapter two), and proceeding to the self-examination and transformation practised in *mahāyāna* Buddhism (chapters three and four). This is followed by an introduction to the role of philosophical investigation in Tibetan Buddhism (chapter five), and to the nature and practices of the *vajrayāna* (chapter six). The last two chapters are about two aspects of the whole path: the function of prayer and other rituals (chapter seven); and the biographies of previous masters as a focus for devotion and inspiration (chapter eight).

The chapters are also roughly chronological (only chapter six is out of chronological order), so I hope they will also give a sense of the progress of the Tibetan Buddhist tradition over more than a millennium – from the time of the Tibetan emperors in the eighth century through to the twentieth century. The twenty-first century is also included, as all of these texts contain teachings that are being put into practice across the world today. Most of the texts are from one of the main schools of Tibetan Buddhism, the Sakya. I have selected these texts in order to give the path they take us on a sense of coherence. Yet they speak to the whole of the tradition as well, something I emphasize by beginning with a text that was written before there were any distinct schools of Tibetan Buddhism, and by ending with the life of the originator of the non-partisan movement in Tibetan Buddhism, who sought to break down false distinctions between the schools.

Every text has a context, and each chapter of this book has an introduction in which I try to provide adequate context for the translation that follows. For a practitioner, the context would be supplied by the teacher, and by the practitioner's own previous experience. The text would usually be heard first in a teaching session, embedded in the commentary of the teacher, or of a previous teacher from the textual lineage. At the least, a ritual of transmission is usually required in which the teacher simply reads the text, sometimes at great speed, to the student. This ritual emphasizes the importance of the lineage of transmission and the fact that even texts are prescriptions given by the teacher to a student, as a doctor prescribes medicine to a patient.[14]

Texts like these are not always easy to understand on the first reading. For one thing, Buddhism incorporates much more than can be explained in a book such as this, and I have therefore annotated the translations where a brief explanation seems helpful. More significantly, however, our modern reading practices are fundamentally different from the traditional way of reading a text in Tibet (and indeed in any pre-modern culture). These are not texts written to be read through once, as a source of information and inspiration, and put away again. They were written to be read slowly and often, to absorb and internalize their messages. This experience, a progressive deepening of understanding, is key to the process of reading Buddhist texts.

CHAPTER TWO

A CODE OF ETHICS

The Ten Virtues

What is it to behave well, rather than badly? This fundamental question of ethics runs through many of the Buddha's teachings. Because Buddhism is not a religion of divine revelation, there is no equivalent to the ten commandments of Christianity. Instead there are a number of different codes of ethical behaviour informed by the basic principle of not hurting others and not becoming so confused that we fail to know when we are hurting others. The text translated in this chapter, A Teaching on the Ten Virtues, *is a formulation of an ethical code that was used during the introduction of Buddhism to Tibet; it is still at the centre of ethical teaching in Tibetan Buddhism today.*

The ten virtues

In the eighth century CE, early Tibetan Buddhists adopted a code of ethics that was popular among the Buddhists of India, a code that enumerated ten kinds of virtuous behaviour. The ten virtues are an ethical code; they form a set of guiding principles and are not tied to a particular vow or ceremony. Tibetan Buddhist monks did, however, take a much larger number of vows, specific to monastic life; and lay Buddhists could adhere to a set of five basic precepts, which were very close in spirit to the ten virtues.

Like ethical codes in many other traditions, the ten virtues are injunctions to avoid certain kinds of physical behaviour, speech, and mental attitudes. Thus they are essentially the avoidance of ten 'non-virtues':

Physical behaviour to avoid:

1. Killing – taking the life of any living creature.
2. Taking what is not given – stealing, whether through force or deceit.
3. Sexual misconduct – inappropriate sexual behaviour.

Speech to avoid:

4. Lying – telling untruths; although some untruths are more serious than others.
5. Provoking discord – causing ill-feeling between two other people.
6. Speaking harshly – causing others to suffer with unkind words.
7. Speaking frivolously – wasting time in pointless conversation.

Mental attitudes to avoid:

8. Malevolent thoughts – wishing ill of somebody.
9. Covetous thoughts – wanting what another person has.
10. Wrong views – holding on to erroneous ideas.

Bringing Buddhism to Tibet

The ten virtues played a foundational role in Tibetan Buddhism from an early stage. The emperor who in the eighth century declared Buddhism to be the state religion of Tibet was Tri Song Detsen (r.756–c.800). When he set out to establish Buddhism in Tibet, he invited the preeminent abbot and scholar Śāntarakṣita to instruct the emperor and his court in the fundamental principles of Buddhism. Based on this, the emperor formulated a vision of Buddhism that he wanted to communicate to his people, which he expressed in this edict:

> The quality of our life depends on our actions. When we do good with our body, speech and mind, we live accordingly. . . . The fruits of what we do to others ripens within ourselves. Rebirth in one of

> the six realms, as a god living in heaven, a human who lives upon the earth, a demigod, hungry ghost, animal, or a denizen of hell beneath the ground, depends entirely on our own actions. Those who have transcended the world are the ones who have become buddhas, bodhisattvas, solitary buddhas, and hearers, and they all achieved this through accumulating merit and wisdom. What then is virtue? It is the ten virtues. What is non-virtue? It is the ten non-virtues.[1]

The Tibetan word translated here as 'actions' is *las*, which in turn translates the Sanskrit *karma*. This reflects an understanding that karma is no more than actions and their effects. The emperor's message, which was no doubt closely based on, if not written by his Indian Buddhist teachers, makes one thing very clear: Happiness and suffering are both within our reach, and whether we experience one or the other is entirely dependent on how we choose to act. This is not true just because the Buddha taught it. It is true because of the inexorable connection between cause and effect.

Before Buddhism came to Tibet, its people, like those in many other cultures, believed that their own happiness was utterly reliant on the whims of unseen beings, gods, spirits, and demons. To be alive was to be in constant negotiation with these entities through rituals. Though these beliefs and rituals never went away, Buddhism offered an alternative. This was the message of the emperor's edict: It is not the capricious whims of unseen beings, but the explicable workings of karma that lie behind the cycle of joy and sorrow that is human life. The edict also mentions the ultimate goal of Buddhism: liberation from habitual patterns and the cycle of birth and death (*saṃsāra*). But the main theme of the emperor's edict was living well, and that is why the ten virtues are central to its message.

In the years that followed, the ideas of karma and of the ethical code embodied in the ten virtues spread throughout the vast reaches of the Tibetan empire. Though the empire would crumble within a century of Tri Song Detsen's edict, the emperors who came after him continued his work. There was a danger that Buddhism would become a court religion, a specialty of the Tibetan aristocracy. Against this, the emperor Senaleg carved in stone an edict stating that Buddhism was for all of the Tibetan people.

There was still a possibility that the Buddha's teachings would remain in central Tibet, never reaching the far corners of the empire. The emperor Ralpachen therefore sent orders that a brief exposition of the ten virtues was to be copied and circulated in every district. Several copies of that text were preserved in Central Asia, in a cave in Dunhuang that was sealed at the beginning of the eleventh century. So there can be no doubt that the code of the ten virtues was key to the Tibetan imperial project of converting Tibet into a Buddhist country. The teaching on the ten virtues translated below is the most likely candidate for the text that was circulated throughout Tibet.[2]

Virtues and vows

Centuries later, when the transformation of Tibet into a Buddhist country was complete, the era of the Tibetan empire was retold in an idealized form, with the memories of the Buddhist emperors assuming mythical proportions. These later stories tell us little about the time of the empire, but they do tell us a great deal about the time when they were written. By the twelfth century, many Tibetans had come to believe that the ideal ruler was one who combined religious and political authority – that 'church' and 'state' should be a single entity. The person who came to embody this union was the first of the great Tibetan emperors, Songtsen Gampo. The way these stories show how Songtsen Gampo combined religious and political power is through the ten virtues.

The stories relate how the text of *A Teaching on the Ten Virtues* was brought to Tibet and that one of the first things Songtsen Gampo did after one of his ministers had created a Tibetan alphabet was to translate this work into Tibetan. The next thing he did was to create the laws by which his new empire would be governed. These laws were based on the ten virtues.[3] Whether or not this story has a basis in reality, it became part of Tibet's foundation mythology.

While it is unlikely that the ten virtues were ever applied directly to a legal case, they did provide the constitutional background for law and governance in Tibet. At the same time, they formed a personal code by which everyone, both monks and laity, could live. The importance of the ten virtues in Tibetan Buddhism can therefore hardly be overstated. They stood at the centre of the union of religious and political rule, and they provided a code of honour that bound the individual to the ideals of society as a whole.

A commitment to the ten virtues is taken by lay people and monks when they accept the *pratimokṣa* vows. These are the basic commitments to ethical behaviour that are the minimal requirements to being considered a Buddhist. In practice, a commitment to the vows is made in the ceremony of taking refuge in the three jewels: the Buddha, the *dharma*, and the *saṅgha*. To take refuge is to become a part of a community (*saṅgha*) that practises the teachings (*dharma*) of the supreme teacher (*buddha*). It is known as 'taking refuge' because to practise the Buddhist path is to be protected from suffering.[4]

The specific vows taken by lay people differ from those taken by monastics. Lay people take five vows: not to kill, steal, lie, engage in sexual misconduct, or become intoxicated. These overlap with the ten virtues, and the practice of the ten virtues is generally accepted as part of the lay *pratimokṣa* vows. The vows for monks and nuns are far more numerous, deriving from the monastic code (*vinaya*) of the Mulasarvāstivāda school of Indian Buddhism. Though there are several hundred specific vows for monastics, the most important commitments are to avoid the 'four defeats' – actions which entail immediate expulsion from the order. These are to kill, steal, have sexual intercourse, or to falsely claim spiritual powers.[5]

Reading the ten virtues

There is no appeal to authority in *A Teaching on the Ten Virtues,* the text translated here. The logic of the text is causation: If you do *x*, then *y* will happen. This is, of course, karma. Every event comes about because of previous events. Moreover, every event sets up chains of causation that produce innumerable further effects. The Buddha's teachings on karma take this insight to a personal level: Everything I do will have effects. In time, I will experience the effects of my own actions – whether in my environment, the people I find around me, or in the gradual changes to my own personality.

Thus the logic of the ten virtues appeals to our interest in our own well being. Don't steal, the text says; not because it's bad in itself, but because bad things will happen to you if you do steal. The way these consequences are described is almost paradoxical. If you steal, you will end up poor. Other, more detailed texts on the ten virtues lay out the thinking behind this. If you steal repeatedly, you are likely to end up in the company of thieves, which makes it more likely that you will be robbed. The same is true of other kinds of behaviour and mental attitude.

In the broader scheme of things, the text also tells us what will happen in lives to come. In *saṃsāra,* life is an endless cycle of birth and death. To be born human is considered a great privilege, as it is only in human life that it is possible to practise the Buddha's teachings. Birth as a human being is attributed to previous virtuous behaviour. Consistently bad behaviour in human life is likely to lead to rebirth in less favourable states of being, the 'three lower realms' the text describes: birth as a denizen of the hells, as a hungry ghost, or as an animal. It is said that these three kinds of rebirth are the result of a preponderance of anger, greed, or stupidity in this human life.

Towards the end of the text, we also hear about rebirth into the higher realms of being. Living a virtuous life is said to lead to a rebirth in a human life, in a position of privilege or wealth. Upholding the ten virtues can even lead to rebirth as the lowest form of god: an attendant in the realms of desire. While the Buddha denied the idea of a permanent, autonomous god, just as he denied that anything could be permanent or autonomous, he did not deny the existence of gods per se. The Indian mythology that Buddhism inherited is full of gods; these gods are just another kind of sentient being, living lives that are long and pleasurable, but must still eventually come to an end.

Thus the practice of virtue can lead to the lowest level of divine rebirth, in the realm of desire. The higher divine realms, those of form and formlessness, are reached through certain kinds of non-Buddhist meditation practice. These are practices of absorption and the shutting-off of sensory perception, and do not lead to enlightenment. Instead, due to the meditator's attachment to the absence of distraction, they lead to the refined mental states of these god realms.

A Teaching on the Ten Virtues ends with a short discussion of meditation in Buddhism according to the approaches of the hearer (*śrāvaka*), the solitary buddha (*pratyekabuddha*), and the bodhisattva. The hearers are those who follow the teachings that the Buddha gave to his first disciples on the noble eightfold path. The solitary buddhas are those who realize for themselves the truth that the Buddha understood when he sat under the bodhi tree: the twelve links of dependent origination. Together, they are considered to belong to the vehicle of the hearers, another name for the *hīnayāna*.

The bodhisattvas, on the other hand, belong to the *mahāyāna* or 'greater vehicle', and their greatness is in their compassion and wisdom. This wisdom is brought about through a meditation that embraces emptiness, which our text calls 'non-abiding'. What this means is that the meditation of the bodhisattva contains no point of reference. It is a process without a fixed end-point, and therefore it does not reach a conclusion; it is 'non-abiding'. Likewise, the wisdom that results from this meditation is non-abiding.[6]

The reason for having this discussion at the end of a teaching on ethical behaviour is that in Buddhism ethical behaviour alone can only take you so far. Practising the ten virtues can lead to happiness, in this life and the next, but it is not sufficient to take you out of the cycle of birth and death. And because nothing is permanent, this happiness will not last. Only through wisdom can we transcend the cyclical alternation of happiness and suffering. When I do a virtuous deed, the wisdom of emptiness sees that neither I, nor the person who is the recipient of the deed, nor the deed itself, have any independent reality. They only exist at this moment in relation to each other – this is what is meant by 'emptiness'.

Rather than abandoning virtue, the bodhisattva does the right thing, but perceives its emptiness. In this way he or she is free from the patterns of thinking that result in the cycle of happiness and suffering, birth and death. Of course, having realized the emptiness of all actions, the bodhisattvas could behave in any way at all. As the text says, whatever they do is equivalent to enlightenment. But since they are compassionate, they act for the benefit of those who do not understand emptiness. And if we look at each of the ten virtues, we can see that all of them are based on the principle of compassion.[7]

Sources for the translation

The text of *A Teaching on the Ten Virtues* was not included in the Tibetan canon. In fact it may already have disappeared from Tibet by the time the canon was compiled in the fourteenth century. The text did survive, however, among the thousands of ancient Tibetan manuscripts discovered in the Dunhuang caves in the early twentieth century. In the collections recovered from this cave, we find five copies of a text on the ten virtues. Judging by their writing style, at least two of them seem to have been written during the Tibetan empire, in the first half of the ninth century. As for the title of this text, one copy calls it *A Teaching on the Ten Virtues* while another has *An Extensive Teaching on the Ten Virtues*.[8]

The origin of the text itself is obscure. It could have been a translation from Sanskrit or Chinese, but it looks more like an original Tibetan composition, as it contains references to hunting and legal practices that draw on the culture of imperial Tibet. The language is archaic, harking back to the imperial period with words and phrases rarely encountered in later Tibetan literature. The language is also a little more direct than usual; the usual term for the second non-virtue is 'taking what is not given', but in *A Teaching on the Ten Virtues* it is simply 'stealing'. Similarly, 'sexual misconduct' is simply 'sex' (though, as the text makes clear, it is not sex in itself that is problematic for lay people).

This text circulated during the Tibetan empire to help educate the Tibetans in the basics of the new state religion. It may have been the text that the emperor Ralpachen commanded to be copied in every corner of his empire. It certainly is an effective introduction to the ethical code of Buddhism, which continued to be the basis for religion and government accepted by Tibetans throughout their history.

TRANSLATION

✦

A TEACHING ON THE TEN VIRTUES

It is said: 'Where there is good behaviour, there are the ten virtues; where there is bad behaviour, there are the ten non-virtues.' What then are the ten non-virtues? These ten are composed of three in body, four in speech, and three in mind. What are the three in body? They are not killing, not taking what has not been given, and not having sex improperly.

1. *Killing* is in three parts: killing because of desire; killing because of hatred; and killing because of ignorance. Of these, 'killing because of desire' means killing due to desire for meat and hide, or for horn and wool, and so on. 'Killing because of hate' means killing another person because of a deep-seated anger towards them. 'Killing because of ignorance' means recognizing virtue and sin, but mistaking one for the other and killing sentient beings. The result of killing is to fall into the three lower realms. Though some may escape that fate and be born as human beings, they will be killed by others, their lives will be short, and they will suffer many illnesses. Those who are able to avoid killing will be reborn as a god or human being. Their lives will be long, they will not suffer illness.
2. *Taking what has not been given* is also in three parts: stealing by force; stealing by trickery; and stealing by smashing and taking. Of these, 'stealing by force' means through extortion, banditry, and the like. 'Stealing by trickery' means such actions as making one's own weights and measures, disputing and rejecting the payment,

then making new ones, selling the goods elsewhere and making a profit. 'Stealing by smashing and taking' means such actions as breaking into someone's house when they are not looking and stealing everything in it. The result of stealing is to fall into the three lower realms. Though some may escape that fate and be born as a human being, they will not be able to hang on to their fields or cattle, which will be stolen by others, or taken by force. Those who are able to avoid stealing completely will be reborn as a god or human being. They will have wealth and resources, and these will not be stolen or taken by force.

3. *Having improper sex* is also in three parts: protected by the *dharma*; protected by the king; and protected by one's father and mother. Of these, 'protected by the *dharma*' means that the *dharma* prohibits sleeping with one's mother, sister, or with animals. 'Protected by the king' means that it is not permissible to have sex with the wife of a ruler. 'Protected by the father and mother' means that for a father, mother, or anyone in a similar role to have totally improper sexual relations with children is not permitted. The result of having improper sex is to fall into the three lower realms. Though some may escape that fate and be born as a human being, they will not be able to hold on to their children, and will fall out with their spouses. Their bodies will be infected with foul diseases, and nothing good will come to them. Those who are able to avoid having improper sex will be reborn as a god or human being. They will be harmonious with their spouses and will hold on to their children. Their bodies will not be infected with foul diseases, and good things will come to them.

The four in speech are not to lie, not to incite discord, not to speak harshly, and not uttering frivolous words.

4. *Lying* is in three parts: lying about being a religious teacher due to one's worldly accomplishments; necessary lying; and unnecessary lying. Of these, lying about being a religious teacher due to one's

worldly accomplishments refers to people such as sorcerers and sorceresses. When vulgar people see their miracles, they don't understand and say 'Look! they're like gods!' Necessary lying means lying because one's life and position are endangered. Unnecessary lying means uttering pointless frivolous speech and speaking untruths. The result of lying is to fall into the three lower realms. Though some may escape that fate and be born as a human being, nobody will trust anything they say, and others will deceive them and make fools of them. Those who are able to avoid lying will be reborn as a god or human being. They will speak wisely and eloquently, and others will put trust in anything they say.

5. *Provoking discord* is when someone is unhappy with the harmonious relationship between two others and speaks words that provoke discord to one of them in order to cause them to argue and separate. The result of provoking discord is to fall into the three lower realms. Though some may escape that fate and be born as a human being, they will not have a harmonious relationship with anyone, and others will seek to create trouble for them. Those who are able to avoid divisive talk will be reborn as a god or human being. They will have harmonious relationships with everyone, and no one will seek to create trouble for them.
6. *Speaking harshly* refers to cutting words or fault finding. The result of speaking harshly is to fall into the three lower realms. Though some may escape that fate and be born as a human being, others will criticize and find fault with them and they will have few servants or bondsmen. Those who are able to avoid speaking harshly will be reborn as a god or human being. They will be liked by all and will have many servants and bondsmen.
7. *Frivolous words* refers to meaningless words of no importance, such as reciting non-Buddhist mantras, telling folktales, or chattering foolishly. The result of frivolous talk is to fall into the three lower realms. Though some may escape that fate and be born as a human being, they will have little wisdom but many words, and will be incompatible with everyone. Those capable of not speaking friv-

olous words will have much wisdom but few words, and will be compatible with everyone.

The three things not to be done with the mind are not to have malevolent thoughts, not to have covetous thoughts, and not to have wrong views.

8. *Malevolent thoughts* refers to malevolent thoughts about the three jewels, or seeing a sentient being and feeling unhappy about his or her good qualities. The result of malevolent thoughts is to fall into the three lower realms. Though some may escape that fate and be born as a human being, they will never come across the three jewels, and other sentient beings will harbour ill will and hatred towards them. Those who are able to avoid malevolent thoughts will be reborn as a god or human being. They will always meet with the three jewels and will be liked by all sentient beings.
9. *Covetous thoughts* refers to craving the qualities of the five objects of desire and craving one's own and others' wealth and property. The result of covetous thoughts is to fall into the three lower realms. Though some may escape that fate and be born as a human being, they will be born at the site of their desire. For example, someone who has coveted women will continue to cycle in *saṃsāra*, and later will be reborn as a louse on the body, or a parasite in the vagina. Those who are able to avoid covetous thoughts will be reborn as a god or human being. They will not have to seek the things they desire but will find whatever they need.
10. *Wrong views* refers to not turning to the three jewels and relying upon them. Within that, not understanding the true nature of the *mahāyāna* – that there is no creation or cessation – is a wrong view. The result of wrong views is to fall into the three lower realms. Though some may escape that fate and be born as a human being, they will not even hear the names of the three jewels, and will cycle for a long time within the suffering of the three realms. Those who

> do not hold wrong views will be reborn as a god or human being. They will always turn to the three jewels and will swiftly progress to full enlightenment.

Those who maintain every part of the ten virtues in an objectifying manner, without the mind of an omniscient one, will be born as a divine attendant inhabiting up to the sixth heaven of the realm of desire. Those who maintain more than half of the ten virtues will be born in the form of an upper-class person such as a king or minister. Those who maintain fewer than half of the ten virtues will be born in the form of a lower-class person. Those who don't practise the ten virtues at all will fall into the three lower realms.

Those who, in addition to practising the ten virtues, cultivate the four worldly meditations in conceptual analysis, happiness, joy, and equanimity will be reborn as long-lived gods in the lower six heavens of the realm of form. Those who go on to cultivate the four formless meditations in limitless consciousness, limitless space, neither existence or nonexistence, and not having the slightest sense-experience, will be reborn as gods of the formless realms. This will last for up to eighty thousand eons. Although they will remain in that state of contemplation for a long time, they will not realize the meaning of the *mahāyāna*. Because of this, they lack the mind of omniscience, and their meditation is objectified. Since objectification entails conditioned virtue, when that merit is exhausted, they will fall into *saṃsāra*'s hell realms.[9]

Furthermore, the three vehicles that transcend the world are those of the hearers and solitary buddhas, and the unsurpassable *mahāyāna*. In the vehicle of the hearers, if they meditate upon the four noble truths, they become *arhats*, and if they meditate on the twelve links of dependent origination, they become solitary buddhas. If they then proceed to cultivate non-abiding meditation, they will attain the state of a bodhisattva and ultimately total enlightenment.

If you are able to engage in this non-abiding meditation, then all lower forms of meditation are included within it, and all teachings are contained within it. Since there is nothing beyond it, this non-abiding meditation is the king of all meditations. If you possess non-abiding wisdom, then whatever you do goes towards accomplishing unsurpassed enlightenment. If you do not possess it, then whatever you do is conditioned, and you are like an unfired clay pot, unsuitable for use.

CHAPTER THREE

✦

HOW TO LIVE

Atiśa's Advice

The text translated in this chapter is a collection of advice on religious practice given by Atiśa, one of the most revered teachers in Tibetan Buddhism. Atiśa's advice is pithy, informal, and uncompromising. Addressing first a lay practitioner and then a monk, he shows that both types of Buddhist cannot rely on the external signifiers of religious life, but must look to their inner understanding, motivation, and compassion.

The role of the teacher

As we saw in the previous chapter, Tibetan Buddhism offers an ethical code as a guide to behaviour. But the practice of Buddhism is not as simple as following a code of behaviour. The ultimate expression of one's character should be one's actions; the role of religious practice, therefore, is personal transformation. In Tibetan Buddhism, as in most Buddhist traditions, this can only be achieved with the guidance of a teacher.

In Tibet, a Buddhist teacher is known as a *lama*, a word that translates the Sanskrit word *guru*. Some books on Tibet refer to all Tibetan monks as lamas, and the term 'Lamaism' is still applied to Tibetan Buddhism, although the term derives from a nineteenth-century view that Tibetan Buddhism is a degenerate form of the religion not worthy of the name. In fact, not all monks are lamas, nor all lamas monks.

A lama is simply a teacher; in the context of tantric practice, a lama is specifically a teacher who is able to confer tantric empowerments (on which see chapter six). Such a teacher must be qualified, but he or she can be either a lay person or a monk, the latter not necessarily being more highly respected than the former. In fact, some of the most revered Tibetan lamas, including the heads of schools, have been lay practitioners. This has led to another myth about Tibetan Buddhism – that many Tibetan monks are married householders. Again, this is the result of confusing the status of lamas and monks.

The role of the teacher is central to Tibetan Buddhist practice. The lama is often compared to a doctor, assessing the nature of the student and prescribing practices appropriate to him or her. These practices are transmitted to the student in a ritualized way. For example, the text of a practice is often transmitted by the teacher reading it aloud to students, and as later chapters describe, tantric practices require further rituals conferring permission and empowerment.

The reading transmission (*lung* in Tibetan) is a way of formalizing the teacher-student relationship, and since each text's lineage of transmission is usually recorded, receiving the reading transmission makes the student part of that lineage. In practice, the teacher often gives a summary of the text, or a commentary upon it, at the same time as giving the transmission. Thus the student receives not just the text, but a way of interpreting it; it is usual for this interpretation also to be considered part of the heritage of a lineage of transmission. If, in the course of their practice, the student returns to the teacher with questions, the teacher answers them with clarification or advice. In the text translated here Atiśa makes this point succinctly:

> What is the point of engaging in a meditation practice just because you have the instructions? Practise in accordance with what your lama says.

Thus, at least ideally, the relationship between teacher and student is a personal one, in terms of practices bestowed, their interpretation, and advice tailored to the student's particular needs. Sometimes these words of advice, or answers to questions, have survived to become textual transmissions themselves, as when students recorded their teacher's words, or when these words were written and sent as letters rather than given in person. These records of personal advice (*zhal gdams*) and answers to questions (*dris lan*) by famous teachers have often been regarded as possessing a value beyond the circumstances in which they were originally spoken.

Atiśa in Tibet

The texts translated here are from a collection of personal advice given by the Indian teacher Atiśa Dīpaṃkara Śrījñāna (980–1054), one of the most revered figures in the Tibetan Buddhist tradition. Atiśa was born in Bengal (in present-day Bangladesh) into a minor royal household. He first practised the *vajrayāna* as a layman, before deciding to become a monk at the age of twenty-nine. In his early thirties he left India to study on the island of Sumatra, where he cultivated the practices of compassion and loving-kindness, and devotion to the deity Tārā. By the time Atiśa returned to India he was forty-five years old. He entered the monastic university of Vikramaśīla, where he gained a reputation as a renowned teacher.[1]

Meanwhile, in Tibet, the rulers of Guge, a small principality in western Tibet, were trying to establish a Buddhist kingdom on the model of the old Tibetan empire, although on a much smaller scale. In this kingdom there were two princes: The elder prince was a warrior, leading the kingdom's armies against its neighbours; the younger son, Jangchub O, was a Buddhist monk. When the elder brother was captured in Kashmir and held to ransom, the younger went on a fundraising expedition to pay off his captors. Unfortunately, by the time Jangchub O had collected enough gold, his brother was dead. Looking for another use for the gold, he decided to fund an expedition to India to invite a famous monk to come and teach in his kingdom. The monk was Atiśa.[2]

A team of five envoys left Tibet for the monastery of Vikramaśīla in 1037, led by the translator Nagtso (1011–64). Braving the heat, poisonous snakes, and treacherous innkeepers after their gold, the expedition eventually made it to the great monastic university. Nagtso and his party settled in to the Tibetan quarters at Vikramaśīla, joining in the curriculum, while at the same time beginning a concerted campaign to persuade the abbot to let Atiśa leave the monastery and travel to Tibet. Eventually gold and diplomacy were successful, and Atiśa was given three years' leave to teach in Tibet.[3]

Half of that time was taken up by the journey to Tibet. When the party presented themselves to the king of the Kathmandu Valley, he insisted that Atiśa stay for a whole year. When the party finally arrived in western Tibet, Atiśa was immediately impressed with the Tibetan ruler's devotion to Buddhism and surprised to see how much translation work had already been done there with visiting Indian scholars. Talking to Jangchub O, he wondered aloud if he was really needed in Tibet. Jangchub O assured Atiśa that there was a great need for his learning.

In particular, the monk prince wanted Atiśa to clarify how the violent and sexual imagery of the tantras accorded with the ethical and philosophical principles of Buddhism. The question had been discussed for generations by Buddhist scholar-meditators in the great universities of India, so Atiśa was well placed to provide an answer. He wrote a brief poem called *Lamp for the Path to Enlightenment,* setting out the whole Buddhist path in graduated stages. This kind of text, teaching the stages of 'the graduated path' (*lam rim*) was to become characteristic of Tibetan Buddhism.

In the *Lamp* Atiśa sets out each stage of practice in turn: the ritual of taking refuge; the motivation of bringing all beings to enlightenment; the meditative practice of calm abiding; the analytical practice of insight; and, based on the nonconceptual wisdom arising from these stages, tantric meditation. He explains how each stage should be approached through a relationship with a genuine teacher.

Atiśa clarified the role of tantric practices among the monks, explaining that, while lay people could receive every kind of empowerment, monks could only receive those that were not related to sexual practices. This, Atiśa said, was based on the teachings of his own gurus, who had believed that the survival of Buddhism depended on the monks, and the monks were only monks as long as they remained celibate. But Atiśa was equally insistent that nobody should criticize tantric Buddhism. Its practices were without doubt the most efficacious, and to belittle them was to belittle the word of the Buddha. Atiśa himself helped to translate tantric texts into Tibetan and wrote extensively in the genre of *vajrayāna* himself.[4]

In order to honour his promise to return to India after three years, Atiśa proceeded to the Tibetan border, accompanied by Nagtso and other disciples. When they reached the border of Nepal, however, they were told that there was fighting nearby and it would be unwise to travel further. While the party waited in their camp, an argument broke out between two of Atiśa's disciples. On one side Nagtso, who had led the party that had brought Atiśa to Tibet, wanted to honour the promise he had made to return him to India after three years. On the other Dromton, a central Tibetan who had recently come to study with Atiśa, thought that there was much more Atiśa could achieve if he travelled to central Tibet.

Given the dangers of travel through Nepal, Atiśa decided there was no fault in agreeing to Dromton's request. It turned out there was much demand for Atiśa in central Tibet, where Buddhist monasteries were flourishing at a level undreamt of in the little kingdom of Guge. While these monasteries had fallen into decline with the crumbling of the Tibetan empire in the ninth century, by the late tenth century a new wave of monks and patrons had moved in, and by the time of Atiśa's visit there were many thriving monasteries with large audiences of monks keen to hear the words of a famous Indian teacher. Along with the work that was going on in western Tibet, this was part of a renaissance that came to be known in Tibet as the 'later diffusion' of Buddhism (*phyi dar*). Seeing the demand for his teachings and the devotion of his disciples, Atiśa stayed on in central Tibet for another ten years. When he died, in 1054, he had spent the last thirteen years of his life teaching in Tibet.[5]

The Kadampas

Atiśa did not found a school, but a number of students built monasteries in which his teachings were practised and from which they spread. Dromton, who had accompanied Atiśa throughout his teaching tours of central Tibet, founded Radreng monastery in 1056, two years after Atiśa's passing. Another student, Ngog Legpai Sherab, founded Sangpu Neutog in 1071. Both monasteries followed Atiśa's principle of combining tantric meditation practice with a firm adherence to the monastic code and with rigorous scholarship. Sangpu monastery in particular became the centre of the renaissance in Tibetan Buddhist scholasticism, with a curriculum covering the four scriptural traditions of the perfection of wisdom (*prajñāpāramitā*), logic (*pramāṇa*), the monastic code (*vinaya*), and philosophy (*abhidharma*). Those who successfully studied all of these topics were given the qualification of *Kazhipa*, 'master of the four scriptural traditions'.

The monks who traced their lineage back to Atiśa came to be known as Kadampas – followers of the Kadam school. The name has many interpretations, but perhaps the most relevant indicates that they taught the Buddha's scriptures (*bka'*) through personal instruction (*gdams*).[6] Throughout the twelfth and thirteenth centuries, the time of their greatest flourishing, Kadam teachers travelled far and wide, expounding the lineage of Atiśa. Tibetan manuscripts by Atiśa and Kadam teachers have even been found in the desert city of Kharakhoto in Inner Mongolia, which was under the rule of the Tangut emperors in the twelfth century.

After the rise of the Sakya school in the thirteenth century, the Kadam gradually diminished, with many Kadam monasteries becoming Sakya monasteries. With the success of the Gelug school in the fifteenth and sixteenth centuries, the Kadam finally disappeared entirely as a school in its own right. The Gelug sometimes styled themselves as 'New Kadampas', but in truth the influence of the Kadam was also strong among the followers of the Sakya school. Some of the most influential teachers of other Tibetan schools – Gorampa of the Karma Kagyu and Longchenpa of the Nyingma – also incorporated the Kadam approach into their teachings. Thus the influence of Atiśa and his students came to be felt in all of the schools of Tibetan Buddhism.

Atiśa's advice

Alongside the literature on the stages of the path deriving from Atiśa's *Lamp for the Path to Enlightenment* and the study of the four scriptural systems, the Kadam are responsible for another major contribution to the landscape of Tibetan Buddhism: the practices known as mind-training or *lojong* (*blo sbyongs*). Mind-training, which draws on earlier Indian *mahāyāna* literature (see the next chapter), is a series of contemplations and mental exercises aimed at reducing the habitual clinging to one's own happiness at the expense of that of others. Atiśa's contribution to the emergence of mind-training in Tibet is said to be his *Jewel Garland of the Bodhisattva,* a work in verse on how to practise the *mahāyāna,* the path of the bodhisattva. This work contains an exhortation to abandon the ten non-virtuous actions (see chapter two), as well as many more examples of how to undermine self-centred thinking and behaviour, such as the following:

> Reveal your own shortcomings, but do not seek out others' errors.
> Conceal your own good qualities, but proclaim those of others.[7]

Inspired by his example, many of Atiśa's students, and students of his students, compiled further mind-training texts. In the next chapter we will look at more formalized mind-training practices. The text translated in this chapter is a more informal collection of advice given by Atiśa on specific occasions. These records of Atiśa's advice, along with the advice of other early Kadam masters, have been passed down through the generations and are held in high esteem for their pithy and no-nonsense approach to questioning one's own motivations and actions. Though not linked to a specific meditation practice, these pieces of advice are intended to inform one's everyday behaviour; it is in this spirit that they have been taught through to the present day.

The two texts translated here are taken from a larger collection, *Sayings of the Kadam Masters,* compiled in the twelfth century. This collection includes advice given by Atiśa, his student Dromton, and other Kadam masters of the next few generations. The two texts are often taught separately from the rest of the collection, as they are considered particularly useful collections of advice. One set is aimed at lay people, the other at monastics. Atiśa's advice implies that while monastics must follow many more rules, the stricture of celibacy being the most obvious, lay practitioners are expected to examine their motivation and behaviour with the same degree of rigour.[8]

In Atiśa's teachings, the most important thing uniting lay and monastic practitioners of Buddhism is the bodhisattva vow. Atiśa's texts translated here, and indeed most of his writing, place the bodhisattva motivation at the heart of practice. The bodhisattva vow can be taken by lay men and women as well as by monks and nuns, and is generally taken subsequent to the *pratimokṣa* vows discussed in the previous chapter. The bodhisattva vow is simpler in that it is a commitment to a single aim: to become a buddha in order to liberate all beings from the sufferings of *saṃsāra*. On the other hand it is considered to be more extensive, both in its aspiration for all beings to achieve enlightenment, and in its duration, which is not just for this life (as the *pratimokṣa* vows are) but through all future lives until the achievement of enlightenment by all.

The tradition of the bodhisattva vow that was brought to Tibet by Atiśa was considered to derive from the bodhisattva Maitreya and to have been propagated by the Indian teacher Asaṅga. Another tradition of the vow, considered to derive from the bodhisattva Mañjuśrī and to have been propagated by the Indian teacher Nāgārjuna, was passed down through the Sakya tradition. The main difference between the two traditions was Atiśa's insistence that only those who have already taken the *pratimokṣa* vows are eligible to take the bodhisattva vow.[9]

The vow itself, made in the presence of a qualified teacher, consists of verses expressing the aspiration to achieve the state of a buddha (*bodhicitta*) for the benefit of all beings. The Tibetan tradition distinguishes two aspects of *bodhicitta*: first the aspiration expressed in this vow; and second, the application of this aspiration in practice. Atiśa, as well as bringing one of the main lineages of the bodhisattva vow to Tibet, is said to have emphasized the aspiration and application of *bodhicitta* in his teachings and to have embodied them in his way of life. Atiśa also expressed the importance of *bodhicitta* in his teachings on the meditation practices of the bodhisattva Tārā, who represents the enlightened activities of putting compassion into practice.

In both of the two collections of advice translated here, Atiśa is more concerned with the practitioner's character than with specific vows and practices. It is said of Atiśa that when he met a stranger, instead of asking after their health, he would ask, 'do you have a kind heart?' The encouragement to look inward and question one's own motivation runs throughout Atiśa's words of advice and is behind such injunctions as: 'Instead of examining the faults of others, examine your own,' and 'It's not the time for guiding students; it's the time for guiding yourself.'[10]

Yet this is not an encouragement to solipsistic navel-gazing; the gradual transformation of one's own character is in the service of the bodhisattva vow. Others of Atiśa's statements concern how to apply the bodhisattva motivation in day-to-day life; for example: 'Have compassion and affection for the lowly and make a special effort to avoid hurting or insulting them.' Thus, while the teachings on the ten virtues in the previous chapter appeal to self-interest in their explication of how one's own actions will affect one's future, the cultivation of virtue in Atiśa's texts is directly linked to increasing the well-being of others.

One other theme runs through both texts: the need to avoid entanglement in day-to-day activities if one is to have the space for internal reflection and considered behaviour. Atiśa addresses various kinds of distractions, including the obviously worldly activities of business and commerce, but also the subtler temptations of praise and respect. In a particularly vivid statement directed towards Jangchub O, Atiśa says, 'Since words of praise and acclaim are beguiling, expel them like snot.'

Atiśa's advice to the layman Jangchub O is uncompromising in its expectations of renunciation of worldly business, rigorous self-criticism, and virtuous behaviour rooted in compassion. Yet his advice to the monks of Yerpa is, if anything, stronger still. This is advice to monastics from a fellow monk who knows that wearing a robe and living in a monastery do not automatically confer the status of a saint. In a technique known as 'putting the finger on the hidden spot', Atiśa tells his audience to ask themselves whether they are genuine monks, or just wearing the robes and living in the monastery while remaining unchanged inside.

In his advice to the monks, Atiśa repeatedly mentions the importance of applying antidotes. These are contemplations applied to specific states of mind. There are various formulations of these antidotes, but the most straightforward are the three that address the three basic negative mental states (often called the 'three poisons'): the mental state of aversion or hatred is countered with the generation of loving-kindness; the state of attachment or desire is countered with contemplation on the impurity of the physical body; and the state of ignorance is countered with contemplation of the interdependence of all things.

The practice of employing antidotes is one of most important ways in which the Buddhist practitioner (whether lay or monastic) proceeds along the path. In a general sense, much of what is taught in Buddhism can be considered an antidote. Yet, while Atiśa has high expectations of his audience, both lay people and monks, he sometimes gives a sense of the freedom gained by letting go of our day-to-day distractions: 'Since ordinary activities never come to an end, let them go and relax.'

TRANSLATION

ATIŚA'S ADVICE

Advice to Jangchub O

After he arrived in Ngari, Jowoje stayed there for two years. Having given many teachings for consideration by Prince Jangchub O, he decided to return to India. Just as he was about to leave, Jangchub O asked him, 'Please grant me one more personal teaching.' Jowo replied that he had already given a great collection of dharma, *but when the prince pleaded with him, he gave this teaching:*

E ma o! It is not fitting that a worthless person like me, with my inferior intellect, should give counsel to friends whose understanding is as high as their thoughts are clear. However, I am inspired by you, a friend whom I treasure in my heart. So, this foolish child will give some motley advice for the sake of a friend.

Friends, until we attain enlightenment, we need to have a lama, so rely on a qualified spiritual guide.

Until you attain the nonconceptual state of being, you need to learn, so listen to the lama's instructions.

You won't achieve buddhahood just by knowing the *dharma,* so practise without being satisfied by knowledge alone.

Always live where virtue is encouraged, a long way from places that disturb your mind.

Until you have achieved mental stability, stay in isolated natural places undisturbed by the hustle and bustle.

Avoid companions who cause negative emotions and hold those who encourage virtue close to your heart.

Since ordinary activities never come to an end, let them go and relax.

Day and night, always dedicate your merit, and stand guard over your own mind.

* * *

What is the point of engaging in a meditation practice just because you have the instructions? Practise in accordance with what your lama says.

If you practise with great commitment, then the result will come very quickly indeed.

For those who act from the heart in accord with the *dharma,* food and clothing come incidentally – this is the way of things.

Friends, desire cannot be satisfied – it is like drinking salt water. So be content!

Pacify and tame the despicable mind that is vain, conceited, proud, and arrogant.

Since what busy people call 'merit' is itself an obstacle to *dharma,* renounce it.

Since gain and respect are the snares of Māra, clear them out of your way like stones in the road.

Since words of praise and acclaim are beguiling, expel them like snot.

Even if comfort, happiness, and friendship are all in abundance at this moment, they are fleeting – turn your back on them.

* * *

In the lives to come, you will need provisions to last a long time; these jewels will grow into a treasury.

Since everything will have to be discarded when you depart this life, be free from occupation and don't be attached to anything.

Have compassion and affection for the lowly and make a special effort to avoid hurting or insulting them.

Practise being without attachment to friends and aversion to enemies.

Instead of feeling envious of those with good qualities, respect them and learn from their qualities.

Instead of examining the faults of others, examine your own and draw out the bad blood of your own faults.

Instead of thinking of your own virtue, think of the virtue of others and practise respecting them as if you were their servant.

Develop the perception that all living beings are your fathers and mothers, and love them as a child does.

With a smiling face and a loving mind, speak calmly and sincerely.

* * *

When irrelevant talk increases, confusion arises; keep it under control and speak moderately.

When meaningless activity increases, spiritual practice is broken; cut off activities that conflict with the *dharma*.

There is no point in becoming exhausted by exerting yourself with hollow activities.

Nothing goes the way we want it to; since everything is governed by our previous actions, it's easier to relax.

* * *

Now listen! For a good person, shame is a kind of death, so be honest and incorruptible.

The joys and sorrows of this life come from our previous actions, so don't blame other people.

Since all happiness is the blessing of the lama, remember his kindness.

Until you tame your own mind, you can't tame other people's, so tame your own mind first.

Until you have clear perception, you won't be able to bring others along, so devote yourself to practice.

The wealth that you are saving will definitely disappear, so don't accumulate sins for the sake of money.

* * *

Since possessions and distractions are hollow, adorn yourself with the virtue of generosity.

To be beautiful in this life and happy in the next, always maintain ethical conduct.

Since anger abounds in these dark times, put on the armour of patience and forbearance.

Those who are ruled by laziness are left behind, so kindle the fire of perseverance.

Since this human life is wasted wandering in distraction, now's the time to use it for meditation.

Guided by false views, you won't understand the true state of being, so investigate its true meaning.

O friends in the murky pool of *saṃsāra,* come to the shore of unborn liberation. Meditating in the way the lama has instructed you, contemplate the river of misery that is *saṃsāra*. Listen to this advice by taking it to heart and not merely repeating it. If you do this, happiness will come to you, and joy to all others too. I ask you only this, please listen to this teaching from my own foolish self.

This was the advice Jowoje gave to Prince Lhatsun Jangchub O.

Advice at Yerpa

When he was staying at Yerpa Drag, Jowoje gave this advice to Yeshe Barwa:

Homage to the conqueror, the noble Tārā. Homage to my sublime lamas.[11]

Noble child, consider well these words of mine. In these dark times, the span of a human life is brief, but there are many things to know. Therefore, since there is no certainty about how long your own life will be, apply yourself earnestly to your own desires.

As long as you act out of concern for your own belongings, like a householder, do not say, 'I am a monk'. If you live in a monastery, but fall into worldly activities and suffer from doubts that you have fallen, do not say, 'I am a monk who lives in a monastery.' As long as you do not stay away from vindictiveness and a fascination for the pleasures of this life, do not say, 'I am a monk who lives in a monastery.' If you live in a monastery, but don't abandon getting involved with lay people, sitting down together with anybody and passing the time in gossip and the talk of householders, do not say, 'I am a monk who lives in a monastery.' If you cannot bear the slightest injury done to you by another, and are unable to be of the slightest help to others, do not say, 'I am a bodhisattva monk.'

If you do talk in that way, you will be telling a great lie to the lay people. Even if they believe that you are what you say, first of all, you won't deceive those whose eyes see everything; second, you cannot deceive the effects of your actions, which will pursue you; and third, you cannot deceive the people who are your brothers or sisters in *dharma*.

* * *

Now, remember what you promised before your deity and lama when you generated the awakening mind. When you come across a situation that requires your forbearance, don't be impatient, saying, 'it's too hard!' Remember not to avoid doing things even if they are difficult. The time for deciding whether it was too difficult was when you took the vow in the first place. Once you have taken the vow, if you fall from it, it is a betrayal of your deity and your lama. So remember, it is not appropriate to avoid doing something just because it is difficult.

The importance of living in a monastery is to give up mixing with lay people and to renounce attachment to your relatives. Once you have renounced these, you will be without all the causes and conditions for thoughts and distractions, such as craving desirable things. As long as you watch over your precious awakening mind, you will not entertain even for a moment those thoughts that lead to worldly activities.

As you have not previously trained in the way of the *dharma* and have weak resolve, worldly thoughts and emotions will come up again and again, and overpower you. Unless you rely on an especially strong antidote to this, it will be meaningless to live in a monastery. You will be just like the birds and animals that live there too. Don't think, 'It's too difficult to do now, I'll do it later.' A precious jewel that slips from the hand of a blind man won't be found again.

* * *

Instead of counting the number of months and years you have spent practising, look at the extent of your conceptualization and the strength of resolve in your own mind. Look at whether you are being hypocritical about your negative emotions. Always keep a watch over your own mind. Don't make yourself miserable. Don't deceive yourself. Don't deceive your deity and lama. Don't ruin yourself, or bring about the ruin of others.

Unprincipled activities in this life and dishonest ways of making a living are a transgression of your vows. If there was a heap of dirt in front of you that you needed to remove quickly, and you could do so with the help of another person, there would be no reason to worry. In the same way, all the thoughts and emotions of this life need to be countered with every single antidote you have. If your lama's special assistance helps you to counter them, what is there to worry about?

Having made a promise before your deity and lama to work for the good of all sentient beings, don't make distinctions between the objects of your generosity. Even if such distinctions do exist, there are no distinctions in the conduct of the awakening mind. If someone harms you, do not be angry towards them. If you get angry, where is your meditation on forbearance? It is important to remember the antidote as soon as a negative emotion appears. What is the point of *dharma* that is abandoned when negative emotions get the upper hand?

Cherish the jewel of your awakening mind. Watch and make sure there are no cracks of forgetfulness, even for a moment. If you allow a crack of forgetfulness, then the Māra of negative emotions will enter through it. Once that happens, your awakening mind will be disrupted. You won't be able to help others, and won't even be able to save yourself from lower rebirths. Keep that in mind! You might say, 'I practise the *dharma*', but this will have become meaningless.

* * *

Noble children! When you die, don't be the cause of grief and dejection in your lama and excellent companions. And don't bring sadness and doubt to lay people who have faith in the *dharma*. You may think, 'I practise the *dharma*', but unless you check again and again whether your mind is in harmony with the Buddha's words, then the *dharma* and the person will be at cross-purposes. Then, at the time of death, you will show none of the signs of having trained the awakening mind, only the signs of lower rebirth, and you will only cause grief and dejection in others.

Thus *dharma* practitioners endowed with the kind of pride that leads them to think, 'I have spent this whole human life in the *dharma*', are living in hypocrisy. If you practise in this way you will end up empty-handed at the time of death. In short, if you live in a monastery without abandoning worldly activities and without turning your mind away from craving desirable things, then you will not gain any benefit from the *dharma*. True guidance in the *dharma* is knowing that 'not engaging in activities' means not breaking your vows in this life and the next. But even that guidance will be of no use if it is just lip-service, deception, and hypocrisy.

So, rely on excellent companions. Don't associate with bad companions. Live without a fixed residence. Don't stay in one place, picking up bad influences. In all you do, be in harmony with the *dharma*. In every activity, apply the antidotes to negative emotions. To behave in this way is the true *dharma*, so put your effort into that. If you occasionally develop a good mental quality, don't become proud of yourself, or you'll fall under the power of Māra.

Stay in remote places, where you can be calm and control yourself. You will then have few desires and will be content. You won't regard your own good qualities or seek out the faults of others. Being without fear or anxiety, you will have little conceptualization. Have good thoughts, thinking always of the *dharma* without being distracted in misguided thoughts. Hold a low position. Accept defeat and give up victory. Hold back anger and develop kindness. Knowing the right amount of everything, be easily satisfied.

Flee from worldly people like a wild animal. Unless you avoid that which is contrary to the *dharma*, you won't be a *dharma* person. Unless you avoid the four kinds of commerce, you won't be a renunciate. Unless you avoid the things you desire, you won't be a monk. If you don't have love and compassion, you won't be a bodhisattva. Unless you abandon activities, you won't be a meditator. Don't be a slave to your desires! In short, having settled in a monastery, if you meditate on the *dharma* alone without multiplying activities, then you will have nothing to regret at the time of death.

Thus he spoke.

* * *

Jowo also said this:

Now, in this dark age, it's not the time to supplicate the rich and influential; it's the time to supplicate your own strength of heart. It's not the time to hold a high position; it's the time to hold a low position. It's not the time to rely on attendants; it's the time to rely on solitude. It's not the time for guiding students; it's the time for guiding yourself. It's not the time to cling to words; it's the time to think about their meaning. It's not the time to go here and there; it's the time to stay in one place.

Thus he spoke.

CHAPTER FOUR

TRAINING THE MIND

Parting from the Four Attachments

*The practices known as 'mind-training' (*lojong *in Tibetan) are taught in all the main schools of Tibetan Buddhism. Mind-training texts are collections of contemplations arranged to form a graduated path starting from the state of an ordinary person and progressing towards buddhahood. The translation in this chapter is a commentary by the Sakya scholar Gorampa Sonam Senge on the classic mind-training text* Parting from the Four Attachments.

The genre of mind-training

Many Tibetan Buddhist teachings state that our minds are fundamentally pure, are already in the state of enlightenment and need not be changed. It is only our conceptual and emotional obstacles that prevent us from knowing this. We can recognize the nature of our minds in every moment, as expressed in this verse by Patrul Rinpoche:

> Unfabricated awareness, the ordinary mind,
> Free and open, the innate *dharmakāya,*
> Can be seen nakedly in this mind right here;
> Let thoughts, its radiance, be freed as they arise.[1]

Rather than being the end of the path, however, that recognition may be the beginning. Our habitual patterns of behaviour mean that a mere experience of the nature of mind will not necessarily change us very much. This verse by Patrul Rinpoche is taken from a letter to his students about how to follow their lama's instructions; he suggests that they must begin by training their minds. This is the usual way: to begin one's meditation practice with a series of contemplations designed to gradually transform the way we think of the world, and our place in it.

Essentially, mind-training texts offer a structured course of meditation practice designed to internalize the key teachings of Buddhism and thus transform one's basic motivations. These teachings, which include impermanence, karma, and suffering, go back to the earliest Buddhist scriptures and are found in all Buddhist traditions. Specific to the Tibetan tradition is, first, the name 'mind-training', and second, the highly focussed and clearly structured nature of the contemplations. The most important antecedent in India for the Tibetan tradition of mind-training is the highly influential *The Way of the Bodhisattva* by the eighth-century monk Śāntideva.

The Way of the Bodhisattva strongly influenced the teachings of Atiśa's master Dharmakīrti, and Atiśa in turn is considered to have brought the mind-training tradition to Tibet. It may be more accurate to say that the mind-training tradition was codified by Atiśa's students and their descendants, which came to be known as the Kadam school. Of the many mind-training texts that were produced in the early Kadam, the *Eight Verses of Mind Training* by Langri Tangpa (1054–93) and the *Seven Points of Mind Training* by Geshe Chekawa (1101–75) were particularly influential. Both are very brief texts that cogently express the contemplative practices of the *mahāyāna* path, and over the following centuries both have been the subject of many much longer commentaries.[2]

The text translated here is from a different tradition of mind-training, that transmitted in the Sakya school. It is known as *Parting from the Four Attachments* and is attributed to the first patriarch of the Sakya school, Sachen Kunga Nyingpo (1092–1158). The four lines of *Parting from the Four Attachments* are said to have been given to Sachen in a vision of the bodhisattva Mañjuśrī at the age of eleven:

Where there is attachment to this life, there is no *dharma* practitioner.
Where there is attachment to *saṃsāra*, there is no renunciation.
Where there is attachment to self-interest, there is no awakening mind.
Where grasping arises, there is no view.[3]

Sachen is said to have realized that these lines can be taken as a very condensed summary of the whole *mahāyāna* path, or more accurately, the path of the perfections (*pāramitāyāna*), which is the non-tantric aspect of the path. The first appearance of these four lines in writing is in a brief work by Sachen's son, the third patriarch of Sakya, Jetsun Dragpa Gyaltsen (1148–1216). An even shorter commentary on the verses was composed by the fourth patriarch, Sakya Paṇḍita (1182–1251).[4]

The first teacher to use the four lines of *Parting from the Four Attachments* as the basis for a detailed course of contemplative practice appears to have been Ngorchen Kunga Zangpo (1382–1456), founder of Ngor Ewam Choden monastery and the Ngor transmission lineage. Ngorchen combined the contemplations found in the Kadam mind-training texts with the graduated structure of the four lines, producing a practice manual that is arguably better structured than the earlier Kadam manuals (an opinion that is expressed in the text translated here).[5]

Ngorchen's students included a number of brilliant scholars, one of whom was Gorampa Sonam Senge (1429–89). Though his writings were extensive and highly respected, they languished in obscurity for several centuries due to the religious and political dominance in central Tibet of the Gelug school. Like many of the greatest Tibetan scholars, Gorampa was born in Kham, the eastern region of Tibet. At the age of ten he asked to be ordained as a monk and began his education in the Sakya tradition. At twenty, he travelled to central Tibet to study with the then current luminaries of the Sakya tradition.

After spending time in several monasteries, Gorampa eventually arrived at Ewam Choden, the newly founded monastery headed by

Ngorchen Kunga Zangpo, and studied with that master and his disciples. He left Ewam Choden after several years, at the age of thirty-two, and spent most of his thirties and forties in teaching and administration at several monasteries. He excelled in this area, establishing new teaching colleges and influential curricula in both *sūtra* and tantra. At the age of fifty-four he returned to Ewam Choden and was appointed abbot, a role that occupied most of the remainder of his life. He passed away at sixty-one.

In Gorampa's lifetime the Sakya school lost the political power it had wielded in the previous century under the patronage of the Mongol empire. Central Tibet was ruled by various petty kings with whom the different Tibetan schools competed for patronage. During this time the adherents of the Gelug school were expanding their influence, and in one example of the sectarian nature of the time, in 1442 the local ruler forced Sakya monks to abandon their own teaching tradition and study under Gelug tutors. In any case, Gorampa was able to teach and compose his works, some of which were highly critical of the philosophical views propounded in the Gelug school.

It was only in the seventeenth century that the Gelug school, with the military backing of the Mongolian army of Gushi Khan, established itself as the dominant force in central Tibet and beyond. The fifth Dalai Lama, now the most powerful religious leader in the land, repressed those schools that had been the main competitors of the Gelug school and banned the circulation of texts that were critical of the school's doctrines. These suppressed books included Gorampa's collected works, among those of many other Sakya scholars. It was only in the early twentieth century that the scattered manuscript versions of Gorampa's writings were collected together and published by the printing house at Derge. This thirteen-volume set is still in print; the text translated here is taken from the eighth volume.[6]

The practice of parting from the four attachments

The four lines of *Parting from the Four Attachments* represent a critique of four forms of attachment, each one increasingly subtle. Since

Gorampa's text is a practical meditation guide or *triyig* (*khrid yig*), he uses the four lines as a structure for a series of meditative contemplations, each to be used as an antidote for one of the four levels of attachment. Gorampa puts these contemplations in the context of a meditation session, which, in the practice that is standard in almost all meditative traditions from Tibet, begins with prayers of taking refuge and generating the awakening mind, and ends with a prayer dedicating any merit achieved through the practice to the enlightenment of all sentient beings.

Birth, impermanence, and death

The first of the four attachments is attachment to the things of this life, which are often enumerated as eight preoccupations: hope for happiness and fear of suffering; hope for fame and fear of notoriety; hope for praise and fear of blame; hope for gain and fear of loss.[7] As antidotes to these, Gorampa offers contemplations on the rarity of being born as a human being and on the fact that this life is impermanent, certainly ending with death, which may occur at any time. The first contemplation focusses on the unlikeliness of being born as a human being, when there are so many other kinds of living beings, some, like insects, far outnumbering humans. Gorampa also mentions two examples of unlikely events as vivid illustrations of this truth: 'It is as unlikely as a dried bean sticking to a wall when thrown against it, or for a turtle to put its head through the hole in a wooden yoke that is being blown around a vast ocean.' The example of the turtle is a popular one, and goes back to the earliest Buddhist literature.[8]

These contemplations on the rarity of human life and its impermanence are intended to provide the motivation to practice. Contemplation of impermanence is considered a particularly powerful technique in the Tibetan tradition and is not limited to the mind-training genre.

There is a third contemplation under this heading – on the results of virtue and non-virtue, the same teaching that appears at greater length in the *Teaching on the Ten Virtues,* the text translated in chapter two. Here it also acts as an antidote to attachment to happiness in this life, through moving the focus to the effects of one's actions upon one's future lives. The appearance of this discussion of the effects of actions (or *karma*) here, in a graduated system of contemplation, allows us to put them into a broader context and illustrates that even standalone texts such as the *Teaching on the Ten Virtues* exist in a wider context.

Suffering

The second attachment is that of a person who has renounced the things of this life but still acts in the hope of better things in the next. This way of thinking could result were one to stop at the level of contemplation of the teachings on the effects of virtuous and non-virtuous actions. Thus in *Parting from the Four Attachments,* the next contemplation is aimed at showing that no form of life is free from suffering, and true renunciation must give up *saṃsāric* existence entirely. This contemplation is a tour through the traditional Indic cosmology of six kinds of rebirth, which are represented pictorially in the 'wheel of life' genre of paintings, typically hung at the entrance to monasteries.

The six realms of rebirth are presented in a traditional and straightforward way here, and no doubt for many Tibetan Buddhists the realms of the hell beings, hungry ghosts, demigods, and gods were understood literally. However, a more sophisticated interpretation of these as essentially mental realms goes back at least as far as the fourth-century Indian scholar Vasubandhu, and was also present in Tibet. Indeed, in Gorampa's text, translated below, we see his argument that the hungry ghosts apprehend the same objects as humans but see them differently.[9]

Loving-kindness, compassion, and the awakening mind

The third attachment is that of a renunciate who has given up the idea of happiness in the cycle of *saṃsāra,* but remains attached to his or her own well-being. The practices directed against this form of attachment are contemplations for developing loving-kindness and compassion, and, ultimately, the truly altruistic motivation known as the awakening mind (*bodhicitta*). The bodhisattva vow, discussed in the previous chapter, is an expression of the *mahāyāna* motivation to achieve the state of a buddha for the benefit of all beings. The forms of contemplation explained in Gorampa's text are the methods taught in the *mahāyāna* for gradually transforming one's character until this motivation is grounded in altruism based on a genuine lack of self-interest.

Like the contemplation on actions and their results, the practices for developing loving-kindness and compassion are based on the concept of multiple lives. In this case, the concept is extended far beyond concern with one's next life, to encompass the never-ending cycle of birth, death, and rebirth that is *saṃsāra*. This perspective is used to create a different attitude to other living beings, placing one's current relationship to them in the perspective of the cycle of rebirth. The logic of this is that the cycle has been going on forever, as there is no beginning to the universe in Buddhist cosmology, and therefore one must have stood in every possible relationship to every other living being at some point.

For this practice, the focus is on the relationship to one's mother, contemplating the care that she took in bearing and raising her child. This is to develop a feeling of gratitude towards one's mother, which in turn generates the wish that she should be happy. This feeling is then extended to people one feels positively towards, such as other relatives and friends, and then to people one feels negatively towards, and finally to all suffering sentient beings. The contemplation on compassion is based on the same gratitude towards one's mother, this time generating the wish that she should be free from suffering. This feeling is also extended until it applies to all living beings.

Thus these two feelings – loving-kindness and compassion; the wish that beings should be happy and free from suffering – are complementary and are almost always practised together. In this tradition of mind-training they are considered the basis for generating the awakening mind. The actual practices associated with the awakening mind are meant to turn the aspiration of the bodhisattva vow into a lived reality by undermining self-centredness. The source for the contemplations known as equalizing oneself and others, and exchanging oneself and others is Śāntideva's *The Way of the Bodhisattva*. Śāntideva wrote:

> When fear and suffering are disliked by me and others equally,
> what is so special about me that I protect myself and not others?[10]

Cultivating this thought – that one's own happiness should not be privileged over that of any other living being – is what is known as equalizing oneself and others. It is sometimes also said that, since the selfish pursuit of one's own happiness inevitably leads to suffering, the approach of equalizing oneself with others actually brings more happiness to oneself as well.

The final practice of the awakening mind is the most radical. Exchanging oneself and others is practised through a meditation known as *tonglen*, meaning 'sending and taking', in which one visualizes sending one's happiness and the results of all one's good deeds to other living beings, and taking on their suffering and the results of their bad deeds in return. This contemplation, cultivated over time, is said to transform self-centredness entirely. Gorampa writes that 'this is the heart of all the practices of the *mahāyāna*, the secret instruction of all the buddhas of the three times'.[11]

Contemplating emptiness

The fourth and final attachment is the most subtle. Gorampa describes it as attachment to the four extremes, which are the views that things are inherently existent, nonexistent, both, or neither. Essentially these are subtle forms of mental grasping at the idea of objective reality (the position of eternalism) or unreality (the position of nihilism). The philosophical refutation of the four extremes belongs to the analytical tradition of the *madhyamaka*, on which Gorampa wrote extensively, and which is discussed in the next chapter. Here, since the text translated in this chapter is for contemplative practice rather than philosophical analysis, Gorampa is concerned with the contemplative aspect of the *madhyamaka*. These two approaches, analytical and meditative, are known in the Sakya tradition as the 'outer' and 'inner' *madhyamaka*, respectively.[12]

Thus the contemplative practices of the inner *madhyamaka* are the means by which we part from the fourth attachment. This contemplation is summarized in the concluding verses to Gorampa's text, thus:

> Everything that appears is my own mind.
> Mind itself is just a bundle of causes and conditions, like an
> illusion.
> This illusion is free from conceptual elaboration.

The way that these three stages of contemplation gradually weaken any kind of grasping at reality can be seen even from this brief description. Gorampa declines to describe them in more detail here, leaving that to the personal instruction of the teacher:

> In these practices, if you do not rely on your lama's personal instruction, but meditate as you please, this is a great source of delusion, and since these practices cannot be understood through the written word alone, I will not elaborate upon them here.

Gorampa's approach, which we have also seen in the advice given by Atiśa, is that the subtleties of meditative practice and the variance between individuals mean that practice should not be based on books alone, but must develop out of a teacher-student relationship. Gorampa also recommends that mind-training is practised alongside guru yoga, a devotional practice focussed on one's teacher and practice lineage.[13]

In between formal meditation sessions, Gorampa advises mindfulness, that is, attention to one's mental state and behaviour. Along with this, he advises that the understanding that all things are like an illusion or a dream should pervade all of one's activities, and that this is the best way to avoid becoming conceited about one's virtuous practices.[14]

A KEY TO THE PROFOUND ESSENTIAL POINTS: A GUIDANCE MANUAL ON THE MIND-TRAINING OF PARTING FROM THE FOUR ATTACHMENTS

To those whose knowledge is like the sky, encompassing all things,
Whose compassion is like the moonlight, crowning living beings,
Whose activities are like a wish-granting jewel, fulfilling wants and needs,
Śākyamuni, the peerless refuge, who grants good fortune to all living beings,
Mañjuśrī, who embodies the wisdom of all the buddhas of the three times,
Avalokiteśvara, who has promised to protect all living beings in the three realms,
And Sakyapa, who in this degenerate age took human form in order to guide beings,
To those whose qualities are difficult to express, I bow down with faith.

For the one who by the strength of accumulated merit has obtained the support of a human body to practise the *dharma*,
Whose wealth and glory has been used to make offerings to the teachings and those who uphold them,
Who, with a wholesome and virtuous mind has asked again and again for answers,

I have spoken this extraordinary advice on the essential points of the *mahāyāna*.[15]

The perfect Buddha, who works for the good of the whole world, without needing to be asked, taught the great corpus of *dharma* in accord with the temperaments, motivations, and latent tendencies of those whom he was teaching. All of it is encompassed by the two categories of the perfections and the *vajrayāna*. The first of these comprises the practice of primarily teaching from the texts on the one hand, and the practice of teaching the essential points through personal instruction on the other.

First, let us look at the textual tradition. Maitreya says in the *Ornament of Realization* that the essential meaning of *The Perfection of Wisdom Sutras* is the graduated path of the eight stages of realization.[16] And in the *Ornament of the Sutras* he says that the intention of the various *sūtras* of the great vehicle is to show that reasoning, faith, and so on, are the stages of the graduated path. Furthermore, in the *Jewel Garland of the Middle Way* the great Ārya Nāgārjuna said:

> Rebirth in the higher realms and liberation are the two things that are to be accomplished. Those who accomplish them must have both faith and wisdom. This is the graduated path to accomplishment.

Āryadeva said:

> Aiming for buddhahood that has abandoned the four errors, we cut the root of negative emotions that obstruct the completion of the way of the bodhisattva. Once you have made yourself a suitable vessel for the ultimate truth, the main practice is being shown the nectar of the ultimate truth; this is the graduated path.[17]

Śāntideva said:

> Based on the support of a human body with freedom and endowments, the essence of the way of the bodhisattva is to practise the six perfections with pure aspiration; this is the graduated path to the accomplishment of buddhahood.

Jowo Atiśa said:

> Those of lesser ability abandon attachment to this life and work for the benefit of the next. Those of medium ability abandon the aim of happiness in *saṃsāra* to work for their own liberation. Those of the greatest ability work to attain buddhahood for the benefit of sentient beings. These three types are the graduated path.

Ārya Candrakīrti said:

> At the stage of an ordinary person, practising compassion, the awakening mind together, one reaches the stage of a noble one. Then, practising the ten perfections, one traverses the ten stages (*bhūmi*). This is the graduated path for accomplishing the three buddha bodies.

The tradition of unerring explication by these masters who have explained the intention of the scriptural collections of the great vehicle is truly miraculous. However, while the textual tradition is to be studied by those who are training their minds, it is not studied in the condensed method presented here.

Now, the second of these two, the practices of the essential points through personal instruction, have appeared in many forms, but two are preeminent: those granted to Jowo Atiśa by Suvarṇadvīpa, and those granted to Lama Sakyapa by Mañjuśrī.

In the former, one contemplates the difficulty of obtaining freedom and endowment; death and impermanence; the cause and effect of actions; and the defects of *saṃsāra*. Through these contemplations, one becomes a suitable basis for the development of the awakening mind.

Then one trains for a long time in the practice of loving-kindness and compassion, before embarking on the main practice, which is primarily meditating on the awakening mind by exchanging oneself for others, and occasionally meditating on the ultimate awakening mind.

The subsidiary practices of this path are: transforming negative circumstances into the path to enlightenment; distilling the entire *dharma* into the practice of a single lifetime; the signs of progress in mind-training; the commitments of mind-training; and the precepts of mind-training. The method of these practices is a path to perfection in which one traverses a great distance in small stages.[18]

In Tibet this was given by Atiśa to Dromton, and nobody else. The latter then taught it to the three precious brothers, and nobody else. From them, it spread far and wide. Among the people of this land of snows, this great path is as well known as the sun and moon. These practices can be studied in the works of Gyalse Chodzongpa and his disciples, and those of the great bodhisattva Zhonnu Gyalchog.[19]

Now we come to the practice received by Lama Sakyapa from Lord Mañjuśrī. Although similar in its essential points to the practices just discussed, it is better in the division of the subject matter and the arrangement of the topics.

When Lama Sakyapa Chenpo Kunga Nyingpo reached his twelfth year, he engaged in the practice of Mañjuśrī. After six months, he had a vision in which Lord Mañjuśrī said to him:

> Where there is attachment to this life, there is no *dharma* practitioner.
> Where there is attachment to *saṃsāra,* there is no renunciation.
> Where there is attachment to self-interest, there is no awakening mind.
> Where grasping arises, there is no view.

With these words, he completely summarized the practice of the perfections. The meaning is this: Parting from attachment to this life, your mind turns toward the *dharma*; parting from attachment to *saṃsāra*, you proceed along the *dharma* path; parting from attachment to self-interest, confusion about the path is cleared away; parting from attachment to the four extremes, confusion arises as wisdom.

Parting from attachment to this life, your mind turns toward the *dharma*

This comprises: (i) the preliminaries, contemplating freedom and endowment, and the difficulty of obtaining human birth; (ii) the main practice, contemplating death and impermanence; (iii) the subsidiary practice, contemplating the cause and effect of actions.

First contemplate freedom and endowment. Sit on a comfortable seat and take refuge in the lama and the three jewels many times. Then say the prayer of the four thoughts that turn the mind towards the *dharma*. Think that you are going to attain buddhahood for the sake of all sentient beings. Then engage in the following contemplations:

In terms of this body with its leisure and endowment, the complete set of eight freedoms and ten endowments is difficult to obtain.[20] In terms of the cause, the practice of virtue is necessary, and virtue is a rare thing in this mind-stream. Thus a human birth is difficult to obtain. In terms of enumeration, in the six realms of living beings there are many more in the lower realms than in the higher realms; this can be seen when you count the number of creatures living in a single pond or woodpile in the summer, which is more than all the human beings in the world. Thus a human birth is difficult to obtain. In terms of examples, it is as unlikely as a dried bean sticking to a wall when thrown against it, or for a turtle to put its head through a wooden yoke that is being blown around a vast ocean. Cultivate the thought that, having somehow obtained freedom and endowment this once, one should not waste it, but make it beneficial for the lives to come.

Second, contemplate death and impermanence. Having gone for refuge and generated the awakening mind as before, engage in the following contemplations:

Nobody, having been born, has been spared the fate of death. Thus I am certain to die. Furthermore, at this very moment I can have no confidence about whether I may die or not; there are many causes of death and few causes of life. Thus I am certain to die. When the time of death comes, nothing can help the person who is dying, since medicine and healing rituals have no power to turn it away. After death, none of your companions or your belongings, nothing apart from the *dharma*, will follow you. Cultivating these thoughts, part from attachment to this life.

This is the principal method of turning the mind towards the *dharma*, so, even when you are eating excellent food, wearing nice clothes, and surrounded by many companions, cultivate this thought: 'At the moment I have these things, but one day I will be separated from them and have to go on alone, so they are meaningless.' Then you will part from attachment to the activities of this life.

Third, contemplate the cause and effects of actions. Having taken refuge and generated the awakening mind as before, contemplate this:

I have obtained the freedoms and endowments that are difficult to find, but as all things are impermanent, I must abandon all non-virtue and accomplish as much virtue as possible before I die. The reason for this is that the fully ripened result of practising the ten non-virtues is birth in the three lower realms. The result that resembles the cause, also known as experience following the cause, is explained as follows: Due to killing, one will have a short life; due to lack of generosity, one will have no wealth, and so on. Action following the cause means that, due to becoming accustomed to any particular non-virtue, one wants to do it again. Since the result in all cases is to fall into the lower realms, there is no opportunity for liberation. The result that acts upon the person is to be born in a land of foul smells and whirling dust storms. In view of this, think of the need to give up non-virtue.

Accordingly, the fully ripened result of the ten virtues is a happy rebirth. The result that resembles the cause is that, through abandoning killing, one has a long life, and so on. The result of action following the cause is that one wants to do the virtuous act again and again. The result that acts upon the person is to be born in a fragrant land. In view of this, think of the need to practise virtue. It is of the utmost importance that you understand these essential points regarding what to give up and what to adopt in your actions, and put this understanding into practice.

Parting from attachment to *saṃsāra*, you proceed along the *dharma* path

This comprises contemplating the defects of the three realms of *saṃsāra*.[21] Having taken refuge and generated the awakening mind as before, contemplate this:

None of the three realms of *saṃsāra* transcend the nature of suffering. Those who live in the hot hells endure sufferings such as having their bodies burned and cut with blades. Those in the cold hells endure sufferings such as having their flesh and bone split and crack due to the intense cold. Those in the neighbouring hells endure sufferings such as being in a pit of burning embers. If suffering like this were to befall my present body, I would not be able to bear it even for a moment. The hungry ghosts endure the fearful sufferings of hunger and thirst, heat and cold, weariness and fear. Animals who live among animals endure the fearful sufferings of being eaten by each other, while those who are distributed among humans suffer from being bound into service and made use of.

Among humans there are sufferings that can be seen here and now, such as the high being brought low, not being able to find what one wants, being confronted with what one does not want, and being separated from friends and relatives. The gods of the realm of desire suffer even more than those who dwell in the hells when the signs of their approaching death appear. And even though the gods of the realms of form and formlessness do not appear to suffer, the time will come when they will fall and have to experience all of the sufferings of the lower realms. Since none of the three realms of *saṃsāra* transcend the nature of suffering, I must abandon *saṃsāra* completely and attain the state of liberation.

If we compare the practices up to this point with the practices of the three types of person taught by Atiśa, they correspond to those of the lesser and medium types. In the teachings of Suvarṇadvīpa, they comprise the four *dharmas* that are the preliminary practice.

Parting from attachment to self-interest, confusion about the path is cleared away

This comprises cultivating (i) loving-kindness, (ii) compassion and (iii) the awakening mind.

To start with loving-kindness, it is not sufficient just to liberate oneself from the sufferings of *saṃsāra,* so contemplate this:

All sentient beings without exception have been my father and mother many times over, and treated me with kindness. Regarding my mother in this life: First she bore me in her womb, then after I was born, she cared for me like a tiny feeble animal. Later, she made sure I always had food and clothing.

Having recalled how kind she was, think that since she has been so kind, you must ensure that she is happy. Then consider other relatives and friends, enemies who have caused you harm, and all those who suffer in the three lower forms of rebirth, have acted as your mother again and again in the endless cycle of *saṃsāra,* and shown you great kindness, and cultivate the development of loving-kindness that wishes for them to be happy.

Second, cultivating compassion: Having recalled the extent of your mother's kindness, consider how important it is for her to be free from suffering and have compassion that she remains in a state of suffering. Consider how good it would be if she could be free from suffering, and think that you will free her from suffering. Recalling that all beings have previously been just as kind, cultivate the compassion that wishes for them all to be free from suffering.

If loving-kindness and compassion do not arise in your mindstream, then no part of the awakening mind can arise there. Since the awakening mind is the root of all *mahāyāna dharma*, it is very important to strive in these two contemplations.

Third, cultivating the awakening mind comprises the awakening mind that aspires, the awakening mind that equalizes oneself with others, and the awakening mind that exchanges oneself and others:

First, contemplate this: It is vital that my kind mothers and fathers throughout the three realms are happy and free from suffering. However, I do not have the power to achieve that at this time. Neither do the great ones of this world, Brahma, Indra, and the rest, nor the hearers and solitary buddhas who have transcended the world. Who can? Only a fully enlightened buddha. Therefore I will attain the status of a fully enlightened buddha for the benefit of all sentient beings, and save my kind fathers and mothers from the ocean of *saṃsāra*.

This is the sole cause of attaining buddhahood. This attitude turns every virtuous act into a cause for buddhahood, which is why it is praised so many times in the *mahāyāna* scriptures.

Next, contemplate equalizing yourself with others: Just as I want to be happy, all sentient beings want to be happy. Therefore I should work for the happiness of all sentient beings in the same way that I work for my own happiness. Just as I want to avoid unhappiness, all sentient beings want to avoid unhappiness. Therefore I should try to dispel the unhappiness of all sentient beings in the same way that I try to dispel my own.

Finally, contemplate exchanging yourself with others. Visualize your mother in front of you, and contemplate as follows: She is so kind, yet she exists in a state of suffering – how sad! May my mother's suffering and all of her non-virtuous actions ripen upon me, so that I experience it instead. May my happiness and all of my virtuous actions ripen upon her, so that she attains buddhahood. Then apply this contemplation to others who are suffering – relatives and friends, other sentient beings who you see and hear of, enemies who have harmed you, and all beings in unfortunate rebirths.

At the end, imagine that you gather up the suffering of all sentient beings and take it upon yourself, and that your own happiness and virtue becomes the cause of all sentient beings gaining whatever temporary things they wish for, and ultimately, buddhahood itself.

This is the heart of all the practices of the *mahāyāna*, the secret instruction of all the buddhas of the three times, so cultivate it. The justification of the practice, scriptural sources, and resolution of doubts about the meditation method are also important, but since there are a great many, I will not elaborate on them here.

All of these practices, from the awakening mind that aspires up to this final contemplation, must be preceded by the preliminaries taught above: going for refuge and generating the awakening mind.[22] In addition, it is also good to practise guru yoga. At the end of every meditation session, conclude it with prayers of dedication. In all other activities of walking, moving around, lying down, or sitting, stay mindful.

Parting from attachment to the four extremes, confusion arises as wisdom

Other traditions of personal instruction teach calm abiding and insight, and within insight, meditation on the lack of self in persons and meditation on the lack of self in phenomena. However, in this tradition we meditate in the following three stages: establishing that all appearances are mind; establishing that mind is illusory; and establishing that illusion has no nature. In between meditation sessions, we practise non-attachment by seeing things as being like an illusion or a dream.

In these practices, if you do not rely on your lama's personal instruction, but meditate as you please, this is a great source of delusion, and since these practices cannot be understood through the written word alone, I will not elaborate upon them here. I will, however, give some advice that may be beneficial at this point.

It is very important not to become conceited when you act virtuously, thinking, 'I performed this virtuous act, and because of these virtues, I am a virtuous person!' On the other hand, it is not a problem to mention without pride that you performed a virtuous act in order to encourage virtue in others. Whenever you perform a virtuous act, or engage in day-to-day worldly activities, if you are mindful that it is like an illusion or a dream, then this will be a cause for distinguishing the view. Therefore it is very important to maintain mindfulness.

In this way, there are four stages of the path. First, working for the benefit of future lives, 'your mind turns towards the *dharma*'. Second, abandoning *saṃsāra* and working towards liberation, 'you proceed along the *dharma* path'. Third, abandoning the aspirations of the *hīnayāna* and practising the *mahāyāna*, 'confusion about the path is cleared away'. Fourth, abandoning all conceptual elaboration that clings to extreme views, and practising the true nature of the natural state, 'confusion arises as wisdom'.

Practise the essentials of the path in this way. In day-to-day life, make your physical activity meaningful by performing prostration and circumambulation, make your verbal activity meaningful by reciting hymns to buddhas and bodhisattvas and by reading the profound *sūtras*, make your mental activity meaningful by cultivating loving-kindness, compassion, and the awakening mind, and make your wealth meaningful by making offerings to the three jewels, paying respect to the monks, and so on. If you combine all of this with pure aspirations, then the achievement of perfect buddhahood with all of the associated stainless qualities is a certainty.

Now I will summarize these points in verse:

A human body which can practise the *dharma* is hard to find,
And since its nature is impermanent, it soon perishes.
Understanding this well, I accept virtue and reject non-virtue;
Applying this carefully is the first stage of the path.

Beings in the endless ocean of *saṃsāra*
Are swallowed up by the sea monster of suffering.
Seeing this, I aspire to the dry land of liberation;
Developing this renunciation is the second stage of the path.

Beings as limitless as the sky have been my father and mother
Again and again; remembering how they have helped me,
With loving-kindness, compassion, and the supreme awakening mind,
Working for their benefit is the third stage of the path.

Everything that appears is my own mind,
Mind itself is just a bundle of causes and conditions, like an illusion,
Understanding that this illusion is free from conceptual elaboration,
Cultivating the natural state is the fourth stage of the path.

Wherever I am, I will make offerings to the three jewels,
Gradually abandon all aspects of non-virtue,
Help the poor and unprotected with generosity,
And combine these acts with prayers of dedication pure of the three spheres;[23]
If I do this, I will surely attain my temporary and ultimate aims.

This summary of the essential points of the *mahāyāna* path I offer to you, patron of the teachings, in fulfilment of a promise, and in the hope that it will be of benefit; through practising it, may you accomplish all your aims.

The lay bodhisattva Ralo Dorje, who, motivated by his undivided faith in the precious teachings, is a sublime patron of those who uphold the teachings, requested some advice, a detailed course of training that would benefit the divine dharma. *In response, the monk of Śākyamuni, Sonam Senge, wrote this in the holy retreat of Dokhar, on the third day of the waxing moon of the Mindrug month. I subsequently provided scriptural citations on the essential points of actions and their results.*[24]

Maṇgalaṃ bhavantu. May there be virtue.

CHAPTER FIVE

THE NATURE OF THINGS

Distinguishing the View

If Buddhism is sometimes called a philosophy, it is because the nature of things (including ourselves) and what we can know about them is often discussed. These discussions can become highly scholastic and sometimes seem abstract, but they remain grounded in the original motivation of the Buddha's teaching: the elimination of suffering. In Tibet, the most influential philosophical movement was the madhyamaka. *The logical arguments of the* madhyamaka *have been used to refute the philosophical positions of both Buddhists and non-Buddhists. They are also considered a means of removing the conceptual obscurations that prevent the perception of things as they truly are. Translated here is a text by Gorampa Sonam Senge that sets out an interpretation of the* madhyamaka *texts of Indian Buddhism that was, and still is, very important for Tibetan Buddhism.*

Dependence and emptiness

An understanding of emptiness (*śūnyatā*) is central to Tibetan Buddhism. Expounded in the *Perfection of Wisdom Sutras* and later defended in the writings of scholars of the *madhyamaka* school, emptiness is the nature of all things. Emptiness is the absence of anything existing permanently or independently in the person (such as the soul) or in the external world (such as atoms). Emptiness is also expressed in the truth that everything comes into being, exists, and passes away in dependence on other things.

The *madhyamaka* begins with the works of Nāgārjuna, who lived in south India in the second century CE. Nāgārjuna was educated in the Buddhist philosophical texts known as *abhidharma*, meaning 'study of the teachings'. The scholars of the *abhidharma* analyzed mental and physical phenomena in great detail, producing lists of the constituents of the body, the mind, and the external world. These scholars made a fundamental distinction between conventional and ultimate truth, that is, between things that exist only in a conventional sense and things that truly exist in an ultimate sense. The only things that exist in the ultimate sense are those that are not composed of other things and are not dependent on other things for their existence. These entities are known as *dharmas*.

For example, a green pot can be smashed into pieces, but even if it is reduced to dust, the colour green will continue to exist. Therefore the colour green truly exists and is called a *dharma*. The pot also cannot be reduced further than the atoms that are its smallest constituents, so atoms are also *dharmas*. Mental factors such as desire, which cannot be reduced to constituents, are also *dharmas*. Of course, in Buddhism everything is impermanent, so even *dharmas* are considered to be transitory, except for the unconditioned *dharmas* of *nirvāṇa* and space.[1]

Early *mahāyāna* scriptures, especially the *Perfection of Wisdom Sutras*, challenged this tendency to reify certain aspects of phenomena by declaring that all *dharmas* are empty, lacking existence even in the transitory sense of the *abhidharma* texts. Nāgārjuna reinforced this challenge to the theory of *dharmas*, using logical arguments showing that no entity can coherently be said to exist in and of itself without being composed of parts or dependent on other things for its existence.

Nāgārjuna concluded that the *dharmas* posited in *abhidharma* literature do not in fact exist, but this was not a kind of nihilism. The impossibility of independent existence does not cancel out the world, because the world is dependently originated (*pratītyasamutpāda*); that is, everything exists in dependence on other things. According to Nāgārjuna, the fact that all things are dependently originated means one can account for the existence of mental and physical phenomena without resorting to theories of independently existing entities such as *dharmas*. Nāgārjuna takes emptiness to be a synonym of dependent origination: 'We explain that anything that is dependently originated is emptiness. As there is no *dharma* that is not dependently originated, there is no *dharma* that is not empty.'[2]

Thus Nāgārjuna did not consider emptiness to be a kind of nothingness. The concept of emptiness points to the lack of independently existing entities, but to become attached to that lack as a truth in itself is a grave error. He argued that the *madhyamaka* refutation of the extreme view of existence needs to be accompanied by the refutation of the other extreme of nonexistence as well.[3]

Nāgārjuna also reinterpreted the *abhidharma* concepts of conventional and ultimate truths. For the *abhidharma* scholars, *dharmas* were ultimately existent, while other things existed as conventions. Nāgārjuna redefined the ultimate truth as the recognition that there are no independently existing *dharmas* at all. For Nāgārjuna, ultimate truth is simply the conventional truth subjected to logical analysis and found to be lacking any independently existing entities. Thus conventional and ultimate are not two different kinds of object, as in the *abhidharma*, but two ways of understanding the same object.

Moreover, understanding the ultimate truth does not contradict conventional truth. Nāgārjuna considered that his arguments against independently existing entities and his presentation of dependent origination provided a refutation of the essentialist theories of *abhidharma* and other Indian philosophical systems, but not of the ordinary use of language. Thus the conventional truth free from these essentialist theories is itself the ultimate truth: 'When ultimate truth is accepted as has been explained, convention is not disrupted; the true is not an object separate from the conventional.'[4]

Madhyamaka in India

Nāgārjuna's writings were hugely influential in the *mahāyāna* Buddhist tradition in India. Some of the most important interpreters of his work were Buddhapālita, Bhāvaviveka, Candrakīrti, and Śāntarakṣita. Buddhapālita, who was active in the sixth century in south India, emphasized the negative arguments in Nāgārjuna's work, taking the view that the role of the *madhyamaka* was to defeat the erroneous views of others, not to establish any position of its own. In this he was supported by a famous verse of Nāgārjuna's: 'If I made an assertion, then that fault would be mine; but since I make no assertion, I have no fault.'[5]

Bhāvaviveka, also known as Bhāvya, was a contemporary of Buddhapālita's, who disagreed with the latter's negative method. Bhāvya believed that the negative method was not sufficient for followers of the *madhyamaka* to engage in debate with those who opposed them both within and outside of the Buddhist tradition. He held that *madhyamaka* arguments do make a positive statement, namely that all *dharmas* lack independent existence and that these arguments should be employed as ways of proving this position. This became one of the most significant divisions in the *madhyamaka*.

Another contribution of Bhāvya's was the idea that the ultimate truth has two aspects. The first is a conceptual ultimate, which results from analysis that refutes independent existence, leaving conventional truth understood as dependently originated. The second is enlightened wisdom that is entirely free from conceptual thought. In this way, Bhāvya dealt with two different presentations of the ultimate truth in philosophical and scriptural sources: those which suggest that the ultimate includes all the concepts of conventional truth except for those involving independent existence; and those in which ultimate truth transcends conceptual thought entirely.

Writing in the seventh century, after both Buddhapālita and Bhāvya, Candrakīrti was aware of the two opposing positions that they put forth. In his commentary on Nāgārjuna's *Root Verses on the Madhyamaka*, he strongly supported Buddhapālita's position that the *madhyamaka* did not put forward any assertions of its own. In his own work, *Entering the Madhyamaka*, Candrakīrti offered a concise and thorough version of Nāgārjuna's negative arguments against independent existence. Rejecting Bhāvya's distinction between two aspects of ultimate truth, he presented the ultimate purely in terms of non-conceptual wisdom. Candrakīrti's arguments against Bhāvya were not particularly influential in India, but would later have a huge influence in Tibet.

The eighth-century scholar Śāntarakṣita bridges the Indian and Tibetan traditions of *madhyamaka*. Śāntarakṣita was born in Bengal and studied Buddhist philosophy extensively in Indian monastic universities before taking up the invitation of the Tibetan emperor Tri Song Detsen to help establish Buddhism in Tibet. His version of the *madhyamaka* incorporated more of the other contemporary movements in Buddhist philosophy, including the Mind Only philosophy of the Yogācāra school and new developments in logic and epistemology.

Śāntarakṣita also increasingly turned the arguments of *madhyamaka* against other Indian philosophical schools. These included the Saṃkhyas, who believed that everything was composed of a primordial substance called *prakṛti*; the theistic beliefs of a variety of Indian religious movements; and the different versions of the self (*ātman*) expounded in movements as diverse as the Jains, Advaita Vedānta, and the Buddhist Personalists (*pudgalavāda*).[6]

In his *Ornament of the Madhyamaka*, which was highly influential in the development of early Tibetan Buddhist scholastics, Śāntarakṣita argued that the conventional truth should be understood in terms of Mind Only, while the ultimate truth was established with classic *madhyamaka* analysis. Śāntarakṣita's student Kamalaśīla was an equally able scholar and continued to propagate and defend his teacher's lineage of *madhyamaka* in Tibet. In particular, Kamalaśīla is remembered for defending the gradual path of practice taught in Indian monastic Buddhism against teachers from the Zen tradition, who were becoming influential at the Tibetan court.[7]

Despite the variety of views that emerged in the discussion of *madhyamaka* by these Indian masters, there was general agreement that the *madhyamaka* analysis could be summarized in terms of the original arguments set out by Nāgārjuna. *Madhyamaka* arguments against 'true' or 'inherent' existence fall into two groups: those that target the concept of a permanent, unitary, autonomous self; and those that target the idea of inherently existing *dharmas*. All of these arguments attack the concept of independent existence as contrary to the principles of logic and at the same time contrary to our experience of the world.

Seven arguments for non-self

Buddhism is known for the doctrine of non-self. It is less well known that only a particular concept of the self is rejected, one that is: (i) permanent and therefore essentially unchanging; (ii) autonomous, and totally self-determined; and (iii) singular, not composed of parts. This concept of self existed in India under the name *ātman* and might be better translated in English as 'soul'. The nonexistence of any such entity was accepted by all Buddhist schools except for the Personalists.

The most famous analysis of the self is in the *Questions of Milinda*, in which the monk Nāgasena, in a discussion with King Milinda, compares the self to a chariot:

> 'Is it the pole that is the chariot?' 'I did not say that.' 'Is it the axle that is the chariot?' 'Certainly not.' 'Is it the wheels, or the framework, or the ropes, or the yoke, or the spokes of the wheels, or the goad that are the chariot?' And to all these he still answered no. 'Then is it all these parts of it that are the chariot?' 'No, Sir.' 'But is there anything outside them that is the chariot?' And still he answered no.[8]

The king finally comes to the conclusion that 'chariot' is just a designation applied to the arrangement of all of those parts together. Thus the ordinary concept of the self is explained as a label that is applied to the bundle of aggregates that form a person. This is the sense in which Buddhists do accept the existence of a self: as a label or a convention.

Many philosophers in India and elsewhere have argued against this view of self as a mere label with the assertion that our strong sense of ourselves as a consistent, self-determined, and separate entity must be based on an actual essence. This philosophical doctrine of self is the target of *madhyamaka* arguments. Candrakīrti explored seven options for the existence of a self, which he presented in terms of the chariot metaphor from the *Questions of Milinda*:

> One does not consider the chariot to be different from its own parts, nor to be identical, nor to be in possession of them. Nor is it in the parts, nor are they in it, nor is it the mere composite or the shape of its parts.[9]

These arguments are meant to exhaust every possible logical argument for the existence of a permanent self. No permanent, singular, and autonomous self is experienced outside of the mental and physical constituents of a person, not even if the relationship is presented in terms of the self owning these constituents or being a container for them. Nor can a singular self be logically defended as being identical with one of these multiple constituents, or contained in one of them, or be identified with them as a whole, or with their shape.

Thus this philosophical self (or soul) is, Candrakīrti argues, not even valid from the point of view of conventional truth. In conventional terms, it is sufficient to take the answer of King Milinda, that a concept of self is a label applied to the various constituents of a person:

> Even though the self must remain unproven according to any of the seven alternatives, either in ultimate truth or in the context of everyday experience, nevertheless, for everyday purposes it is designated in dependence on its parts, without analysis.[10]

Here, 'without analysis' means that no philosophical justification is required for our everyday sense of self. Nor did the Buddha mean to negate this everyday experience. All that is lost is the idea that the fact of subjective experience, and the language that separates 'me' from 'you', is based on the actual existence of permanent and autonomous entities. This refutation of the idea of a permanent self or soul clears the way for the loosening of the bonds of egotism or 'self-clinging' through meditation practice.

The emptiness of *dharmas*

Further analysis of the self in terms of *madhyamaka* arguments leads to an understanding that the aggregates collectively labelled 'self' are themselves empty, and this is the ultimate truth. The refutation of the concept of inherently existing entities is often presented in terms of five arguments. This list of five, which became popular in Tibet due to its inclusion in Kamalaśīla's *Illumination of the Madhyamaka*, brings together classic arguments from various Indian *madhyamaka* texts.

The diamond slivers

The first classic argument against inherent existence is known as 'the diamond slivers'. It appears in Nāgārjuna's *Root Verses on the Madhyamaka* and more extensively in Candrakīrti's *Entering the Madhyamaka*. According to this argument, an entity that exists entirely independently has to come into being at some point. Nāgārjuna argued that it can only be produced in these four ways: (i) with itself as the cause; (ii) with an entity entirely other than it as the cause; (iii) from both of these combined; or (iv) without a cause. The vital concepts in this argument are identity and difference.

The argument against the first position, that an inherently existent thing is its own cause, is that this is logically impossible: An object that has come into existence cannot come into existence again. It also contradicts our ordinary experiences of the way things develop and change. Even if it were logically possible for inherently existent things to reproduce themselves continually, this would result in stasis. Seeds would never grow into sprouts; instead, as Candrakīrti puts it, 'the seed would reproduce itself until the end of all existence'.[11]

The second position is that an inherently existent entity can be brought into being by an entirely different entity. Against this it is argued that if causes and effects are both independent entities, then anything could be brought into being by anything else, for instance (in

Candrakīrti's example), pitch darkness from flames. The third position is a combination of the first two and is refuted with the same arguments. The fourth position, which rejects causation entirely, is refuted from the point of view of ordinary experience; a lack of causation would result in a world very different from our own, as Candrakīrti says:

> If production is believed to take place in the absence of a cause, then it follows that anything could be produced anywhere at any time, and hundreds of seeds sown by common people for the purpose of raising crops would result in no harvest whatsoever.[12]

According to the *madhyamaka* tradition, these four alternative theories represent all the possible logical defences of the concept of independent existence. The result of this analysis is to refute the concept of independent existence without positing any theory to replace it.

Arising and cessation from existent and nonexistent causes

The second argument is directed against the concept of causes and effects having independent existence. If they do, then there are two logical possibilities: either the cause ceases the moment the effect appears, or the cause continues to exist so that it overlaps with the effect. In the first case, since the cause must be nonexistent before the effect comes into being, there can be no connection between them, so the cause cannot function as a cause. In the second case, since the cause exists simultaneously with the effect, there is no logical justification for referring to it as a cause, as it does not come before the effect.

These arguments are not meant to negate the ordinary uses of the words 'cause' and 'effect', rather they are aimed at dispelling the misapprehension that the cause and the effect are separate, independent entities. The only remaining alternative is that everything comes into being interdependently, and therefore has no independent existence. Cause and effect are merely labels imposed upon interdependent phenomena.

Arising and cessation from the four extremes

This argument is a continuation of the previous refutation of independently existing causes and results. Four possibilities are examined: a single result arising from a single cause; many results arising from a single cause; a single result arising from many causes; and many results arising from many causes. The arguments against these scenarios are based on the previous argument that independent entities cannot have a cause-effect relationship to each other, and the argument explained below – that neither singularity nor multiplicity are tenable if one posits independent existence.

Neither one nor many

Though it goes back to Nāgārjuna, the classic form of the argument known as 'neither one nor many' was written by Śāntarakṣita in his *Ornament of the Middle Way*. Śāntarakṣita used this argument against a variety of Buddhist and non-Buddhist schools of thought. He argued that the concept of an indivisible entity (the 'one' of the argument), which was central to these schools of thought, could be refuted through logical analysis.

If the external world is considered to be composed of atoms, which are the building blocks of matter, then these atoms must be logically indivisible; otherwise they could be split into component parts, and those parts could be further split, and so on. Yet no material object can be logically indivisible, since if it has extension in space, it must have edges, sides, a centre, and so on, and therefore must be logically divisible. In the *abhidharma* the internal world of consciousness is also considered to be composed of indivisible parts, in this case, a series of moments. The same kind of refutation is applied to these moments: since they must have duration in time, however brief, they cannot be logically defended as indivisible.

The 'neither one nor many' argument was also used against followers of the Buddhist Mind Only philosophy. Against the idea that mind is a singular entity, Śāntarakṣita argued that a consciousness that is singular cannot apprehend a multiplicity of objects. Having established the logical incoherence of the concept of an indivisibly singular entity, this argument is turned against the concept of multiplicity; for multiplicity is an aggregate of many singular things. And since being one or many are the only two logical alternatives for an entity that exists independently, such existence cannot be logically established.

Dependent origination

Having established that independent existence is logically untenable, the final *madhyamaka* argument is that the only remaining explanation for phenomena as we know them is that things arise in dependence upon others. This is known as dependent origination. Things have no self-established reality, just as a moon's reflection in a pond depends on the moonlight, the pond, and the person who perceives the reflection. All phenomena are like the reflection of the moon because they only appear as they do in dependence on conditions.

Because emptiness is the lack of independent existence, dependent origination is considered by Nāgārjuna, and by most who followed, as synonymous with emptiness. This identification of dependent origination with emptiness has a negative and a positive effect. On the negative side, it means that dependent origination as a principle is empty; that is, it is not to be thought of as an independent entity or *dharma*. On the positive side, it means that emptiness is dependent origination; that is, emptiness is not just the absence of independent entities, it is also the presence of dependently arising phenomena.

Madhyamaka in Tibet

In its early centuries, the dominant influence on Tibetan *madhyamaka* was the work of Śāntarakṣita and Kamalaśīla. This began to change in the Tibetan renaissance of the eleventh century, with the founding of the monastery of Sangpu Neutog by the Kadam monk Ngog Legpai Sherab. Here Chapa Chokyi Senge (1109–69) taught the *madhyamaka* in the tradition of Śāntarakṣita. But another scholar at Sangpu, Patsab Nyima Drag (b. 1055), travelled to Kashmir and translated

Candrakīrti's *Entering the Madhyamaka*, returning to teach Candrakīrti's version of the *madhyamaka*, along with his criticisms of Bhāvya and, by implication, of those who had followed Bhāvya, such as Śāntarakṣita and Kamalaśīla.

Soon these two streams of *madhyamaka*, which had never been given names in India, were being called *svātantrika* and *prāsaṅgika* by Tibetans. The name *svātantrika* refers to the way Bhāvya and his followers establish emptiness with their own arguments, while the name *prāsaṅgika* refers to the way that Candrakīrti and his followers intended their opponents' arguments to be refuted by pointing out their own logical consequences. The second patriarch of the Sakya school, Sonam Tsemo (1141–82), studied both *svātantrika* and *prāsaṅgika* presentations of *madhyamaka* during his time at Sangpu Neutog monastery, incorporating both into his own work.[13]

As described in the previous chapter, Gorampa Sonam Senge (1429–89) was one of the leading lights of Sakya scholarship in the golden age of Tibetan scholasticism. He wrote several texts on the *madhyamaka*, of which *Distinguishing the View* has been the most popular. Gorampa called the version of *madhyamaka* that he presents in his own works '*madhyamaka* beyond extremes' and in *Distinguishing the View* he claims this as the true intention of Nāgārjuna and his successors.

In Gorampa's time there had been further developments in Tibetan *madhyamaka* thought, which he felt needed to be refuted. These were the 'empty of other' or *zhentong* (*gzhan stong*), exemplified by Dolpopa Sherab Gyaltsen (1292–1361), and the new interpretations of *prāsaṅgika* by Tsongkhapa Lozang Dragpa (1357–1419). Gorampa characterized these as two extreme interpretations of *madhyamaka*, Dolpopa's being eternalist and Tsongkhapa's being nihilist. The polemical chapters of *Distinguishing the View*, which are not translated here, give detailed arguments against specific points in the works of Dolpopa and Tsongkhapa, with the latter coming in for the bulk of Gorampa's criticism.[14]

Gorampa describes his own view as culminating in a realization of emptiness that is itself free from the four conceptual extremes. That is to say, it is not enough simply to refute independent existence, as he states in the introduction to *Distinguishing the View*:

> Having refuted that, one may grasp at the emptiness of true existence. When mounting a horse from the right, one doesn't fall off on that side, but falls off on the left. Likewise, one may not escape from falling into the extreme of nihilism, so this needs to be refuted as well. Furthermore, grasping at both or neither also needs to be refuted, until no object grasped according to the four extremes can be found at all.

Thus it is not sufficient to refute independent existence (which Gorampa usually calls 'true existence'). What Gorampa is saying here is based on Nāgārjuna's own statements that assertions of existence, nonexistence, both, or neither, are all errors rejected by the *madhyamaka*. One must therefore give up not only grasping existence (the first of the four extremes) but also grasping nonexistence (the second extreme), a combination of both (the third extreme), or an assertion that neither are true (the fourth extreme). Thus any view that can be characterized as eternalist, nihilist, or some combination of the two, must be rejected. Gorampa differed from Tsongkhapa in considering it necessary to be free from all four extreme views simultaneously, in a state entirely transcending conceptualization.

The arguments of *Distinguishing the View*

The text translated here probably demands more from the reader than any other in this book. Tibetan philosophers such as Gorampa were writing for an educated audience, one that already understood the basic arguments of the *madhyamaka* and other philosophical schools. Works like this one were written to establish the correct interpretation of *madhyamaka* and refute erroneous understandings of emptiness, the two truths, and other key *madhyamaka* concepts. Reading Gorampa's text requires concentration and patience: more than one reading is very likely necessary. The reward for this effort is that the text places the reader right in the middle of the issues and debates current in the golden age of Tibetan Buddhist philosophy, issues that are still being debated today.

Gorampa begins his explanation of '*madhyamaka* beyond extremes' with an important point. The arguments put forward in *madhyamaka* texts are aimed at those who hold religious/philosophical positions that could be called 'realist'. These include non-Buddhists who believe in a soul or creator god, as well as Buddhists who believe in the existence of *dharmas* or consciousness. Those who don't adhere to any such view do not need to read these arguments; instead, they can turn to meditation practices that establish emptiness directly, such as the practice mentioned by Gorampa in the mind-training text in the previous chapter.

As the basis for understanding *madhyamaka*, Gorampa explains his particular understanding of the two truths, which is influenced by his Indian predecessors. Following Candrakīrti, he defines conventional truth as simply the ordinary practices of society – how things are perceived and named in day-to-day life:

> If somebody asks how we justify our assertion that sprouts grow from seeds, we say this: A sprout growing from a seed is perceived in the mind, and subsequent to that perception a designation is applied. That is all. If they use other kinds of justification such as arising from self, or arising from another, we have arguments that refute these and establish the essential point that further justification for sprouts growing from seeds cannot be found.

This acceptance of perception and language, and the rejection of any kind of justification for it, is not a ban on finding out more about the world. Rather it is a refusal to engage in philosophical speculation about the world – that it is based on an eternal substance, created by a god, or consciousness, and the like. Thus the *madhyamaka* arguments are not tools for explaining the perceptions and language of ordinary life, nor for denying their existence. They are specifically designed to refute religio-philosophical justifications for the self and phenomena.

Ultimate truth, as mentioned earlier, is the nature of conventional truth when it is analyzed and found to be free of independently existing *dharmas* or a permanent, singular, autonomous self. Another aspect of Gorampa's *madhyamaka*, which he inherited from Bhāvya and Śāntarakṣita, is the idea that there are two levels of ultimate truth: an approximate ultimate truth, which is understood through analysis; and a definitive ultimate truth, which can only be perceived through meditation. Gorampa also refers to these two as the 'categorizable' and 'uncategorizable' levels of ultimate truth.

What is the difference between these two levels of ultimate truth? The analytical tradition of the *madhyamaka* texts leads only as far as the approximate ultimate. As Gorampa puts it, 'one cannot transcend grasping using only conceptualization'.[15] Analysis can refute the four extremes one by one, but cannot transcend them all simultaneously; it is in the context of meditative realization that the four extremes can be completely transcended in a state beyond conceptual elaboration. This is the definitive ultimate truth.

As Gorampa argues at some length in *Distinguishing the View*, the approximate ultimate truth can be understood by followers of the *hīnayāna*, but the definitive ultimate truth is realized only by those on the *mahāyāna* path. The two kinds of *hīnayāna* practitioner, hearers and solitary buddhas, both understand the lack of true existence in persons and *dharmas*. What they fail to understand is the other three of the four extremes, i.e. that one cannot impute a lack of true existence either (or a combination of both, or an assertion of neither). Thus an understanding of the lack of true existence (that is, emptiness) is part of all Buddhist paths, but it is only in *madhyamaka* that one arrives at a realization free from the four extremes of true existence, nonexistence, both, and neither.

Furthermore, it is only through the *madhyamaka* that one can overcome the cognitive obstacles to enlightenment. These are one of the two factors that obscure one's inherent enlightened nature: obscuration by the afflictions; and obscuration by cognition. The first of these, obscuration by the afflictions, refers to the negative emotional aspects of ordinary existence, the most pervasive of which are ignorance, attachment, and aversion. These are overcome by various antidotes, including understanding the lack of a permanent self. The second, obscuration by cognition, refers to the imputation of true existence that is the target of *madhyamaka* analysis. The latter is only completely removed by transcending the four extremes, and therefore enlightenment is only reached through the *mahāyāna*.

Gorampa's discussion of how emptiness is understood in the *hīnayāna* and the *mahāyāna* may seem obscure, but it was important for Tibetan scholars to understand what was special about the *madhyamaka*. The usual presentation of the followers of the *hīnayāna* is that they understand the lack of a permanent self by dividing it up into the aggregates (as we saw in the *Questions of Milinda*), but they still believe in the true existence of the aggregates. However, scholars such as Gorampa knew that this was an oversimplification and that the emptiness of *dharmas* was also discussed in *hīnayāna* sources. Thus he came to his position that the *madhyamaka* was not distinguished by emptiness per se (as he says in the text here, the word 'emptiness' is used in different Buddhist traditions in different ways) but by the transcendence of the four extremes.[16]

We have seen how Gorampa insists that the transcendence of the four extremes is a non-conceptual state, and that this non-conceptual realization of the definitive ultimate truth is realized through meditation rather than analysis. We should understand this in the context of the Tibetan Buddhist tradition as a whole, in which those who study and write *madhyamaka* texts are almost always involved in meditative practices as well. Gorampa says much the same at the very end of the text translated here. An awareness that is without conceptual elaboration is the basis and the result of *vajrayāna* systems of practice such as *dzogchen*, *mahāmudrā*, and *lamdre*. Although Gorampa does nor refer specifically to such practices here, his readers would have understood this.

DISTINGUISHING THE VIEW: MOONLIGHT UPON THE ESSENTIAL POINTS OF THE SUPREME VEHICLE

1. Identifying the student to whom reality is taught

There are two kinds of students who can be taught *madhyamaka* philosophy: Buddhists or non-Buddhists who initially hold a realist view, but later change their philosophical position; and those who seek from the outset to understand reality through realizing the potential of the *mahāyāna*.

1.1. Buddhists or non-Buddhists who initially hold a realist view, but later change their philosophical position

Those non-Buddhists who change their philosophical positions have their misconceptions refuted by the arguments taught in the texts of the *madhyamaka* and logic. Abandoning their philosophical views they become suitable students for teaching the *madhyamaka* view. Among the Buddhists there are some who have a realist philosophy: the two schools of hearers, who assert that atoms are truly existent. Their views are refuted by the arguments that appear in the texts of the Mind Only school. However, the followers of Mind Only have a residual clinging to consciousness, which in turn is disproved by arguments such as 'neither one nor many'. They then become students who can be taught the *madhyamaka* view.[17]

When teaching the *madhyamaka* view to realists (Buddhist or non-Buddhist), the *prāsaṅgikas* use consequential arguments to reveal the internal contradictions in their statements. The *svātantrikas* say that it is also necessary to use logical arguments to make them understand the point that is to be proven. Most of the arguments found in their texts are intended for this purpose.

1.2. Those who seek from the outset to understand reality through realizing the potential of the mahāyāna

It is appropriate to teach this second kind of student by guiding them from the beginning in the meditations on personal non-self and the non-self of *dharmas*. It is pointless to make them study two positions and then engage in debate. This second kind of student is referred to in passages such as, 'hearing about emptiness even as an ordinary person', and 'the profound doctrine terrifies those who have doubts'. On the other hand, if they do not understand the purpose of this meditation practice, then the arguments that are explained in the texts should be taught to them in detail.

2. The state of reality

I will explain this according to a threefold distinction that has been made by previous scholars: base *madhyamaka* – the union of the two truths; path *madhyamaka* – the union of the two accumulations; and result *madhyamaka* – the union of the two buddha bodies.

2.1. Base madhyamaka*: the union of the two truths*

This is in two parts: a presentation of the conventional, and a presentation of the ultimate.

2.1.1. The conventional

If you have previously followed one of the two philosophical schools of the hearers and then become a follower of the *madhyamaka* without ever developing the Mind Only view, you will accept external objects as mere designations, but you will not accept that they can withstand rational analysis.[18]

If you previously held the Mind Only view before becoming a follower of the *madhyamaka,* you will accept that appearances – as designations – are mental, but you will not accept that they can withstand rational analysis.

If you become a follower of the *madhyamaka* straight away without having previously followed any realist philosophy, then your definition of designations will follow that of the glorious Candrakīrti, accepting them just as they are known by society, without investigating them.

By 'without investigating them' we mean that we do not apply rational arguments that analyze reality. It does not mean refusing to apply conventional designations. Such designations evaluate identity and existence, and so on, and it is necessary to categorize things in this way before accepting them. Those few people who have said that we should reject existence and nonexistence, even in the definition of such designations, are not following the intention of the texts. In the context of these designations it is necessary to accept the distinction that rice seeds produce rice sprouts and not barley sprouts; and that fire is hot and burning, while water is neither. On the other hand, in the context of analyzing reality we do not make these distinctions, as we know from the refuting arguments that things can arise from other things.

Defining the conventional as it is known by society refers to what is perceived in the mind of a person in society who is not affected by some incidental cause of confusion, and the subsequent labelling that follows that perception. We accept these conventional designations – 'it is this' and 'it is not that' – just as they are used, without looking for any other kind of justification. For example, if somebody asks how we justify our assertion that sprouts grow from seeds, we say this: A sprout growing from a seed is perceived by the mind, and subsequent to that perception a designation is applied. That is all. If they use other kinds of justification, such as arising from self, or arising from another, we have arguments that refute these and establish the essential point that further justification for sprouts growing from seeds cannot be found.

Equally, there is no other justification for the way that actions give rise to effects except that this is how it is perceived by the mind. If you look for another form of justification, there are only two options: either the effect arises after contact with the cause, or without any contact between them. In the first case there would be permanence; in the latter, anything could arise from anything else. This is clearly problematic. In order to avoid the second problem, the realists posit a basis for actions and their effects.

Tsongkhapa's idea that 'destruction as a *dharma*' is the basis for actions and their effects is no better. When I am analyzing whether there is contact or not, I cannot even posit that effects arise from actions, so what's the point of asserting a basis for actions and their effects? So give up conversations rehashing old disputes about whether this is the intention of the glorious Candrakīrti or not! Investigate the root text and commentary of *Entering the Madhyamaka* with an open mind.[19]

Similarly, when the visual consciousness of a human sees a cup full of water, there is water there because water is perceived in that consciousness. There is no pus and blood there because pus and blood are not perceived.

— 'How is it that blood and pus are there when a hungry ghost is looking at it?'

As in the previous case, from the point of view of their visual consciousness, there is blood and pus there and not water. From the point of view of a visual consciousness different from both of the above, neither of these two are there. It is important to understand this.[20]

2.1.2. The ultimate

This is twofold: the approximate ultimate truth, which is based on rational analysis; and the definitive ultimate truth, which is perceived without elaboration in the meditative state of a noble one.

2.1.2.1. The approximate ultimate truth
The Way of the Bodhisattva says:

> This grasping at true existence is the cause of suffering and should be stopped. In *Praise for the Space of Reality* it says 'As long as one grasps at "I" and "mine", one imagines an external world. When one sees the two kinds of non-self, the seeds of ordinary existence are eliminated.'

As it says, grasping at the true existence of *dharmas* produces grasping at the true existence of the person, and that is the root of all of our problems. This is why the object of these two forms of grasping needs to be refuted through argument. At this point the lack of true existence in persons and *dharmas* is accepted provisionally, for one cannot transcend grasping using only conceptualization. This is because a mind understanding the lack of true existence in this way involves conceptualization that identifies words with their referents.[21]

According to *madhyamaka* texts there are five arguments that establish the lack of true existence in *dharmas*:

1. The diamond slivers
2. Arising and cessation from existent and nonexistent causes
3. Arising and cessation from the four extremes
4. Neither one nor many
5. Dependent origination

These arguments are taken by *svātantrikas* as syllogistic proofs. *Prāsaṅgikas*, on the other hand, take them merely as a way of arguing that will be accepted by others. The arguments that establish the lack of true existence of the person show seven ways that it cannot be found in the aggregates: being the same as them, being different from them, and so on. The most extensive presentation of this is in *Entering the Madhyamaka*.

When one refutes true existence in this way, one is still apprehending the lack of true existence through conceptualization. Subsequently that very grasping at lack of true existence needs to be eliminated; this emptiness should not be taken to be a kind of truth in itself, as neither true existence as the object of negation, nor emptiness as that which negates it, can be established. Based on this reasoning, it is equally wrong to grasp both emptiness and non-emptiness of true existence simultaneously, since it is wrong to grasp at them individually, and a denial of both of them cannot be established.

Therefore, if we do not develop an awareness of how to analyze reality, it will not be possible to apprehend it. As we know from the arguments that refute true existence, this awareness precludes any of the four extremes. So, the essential point is that we need to refute all grasping at the four extremes.

— 'In that case, true existence must be established in the awareness that analyzes reality, since the emptiness of true existence is not established there.'

This has been shown to be wrong in the past, as it represents the system of one of the noble Nāgārjuna's opponents, that the law of double negation applies to this awareness.

— 'Actually, you are contradicting Nāgārjuna's *Sixty Reasons,* in which he states that if you deny that something lacks an intrinsic nature, you will be affirming an intrinsic nature.'

Where is the contradiction? This passage is about the conventional level, where if there is no lack of intrinsic nature, there must be an intrinsic nature. In the conventional context we do not say that things are neither existent nor nonexistent.[22]

In short, no thinking that involves analyzing reality can transcend conceptualization that identifies words with their referents. Whichever of the four extremes it apprehends, it cannot refute them all simultaneously. However, it does refute the four kinds of elaboration one at a time, as they appear. Freedom from the elaboration of the four extremes – which are the targets of these refutations – is said to be the ultimate in the context of a mind grasping at true existence. However, in the context of the meditative perception of a sage, it is still a conventional truth. That is why it is known as a categorizable ultimate truth, or an approximate ultimate.

2.1.2.2. The definitive ultimate truth

Ordinary people refute the elaborations of each of the four extremes one by one. Then they meditate until the *mahāyāna* path of seeing arises. At that point, the elaborations of the four extremes are negated simultaneously, and no difference is perceived between the nature of what is realized and the mind that realizes it. That object manifesting inseparably from the mind and free from elaboration is given the label 'ultimate truth'. However, at this point there is not the slightest grasping at the thought, 'this is the ultimate truth'. It is with this in mind that the scriptures and treatises speak of seeing by means of non-seeing and perceiving by means of non-perception.

— 'Doesn't this contradict the fact that emptiness is spoken of as the ultimate truth?'

Well, *emptiness* is merely a label, which is used in many contexts:

- The two hearer schools use the term *emptiness* for the emptiness of self in the person. This is expressed in the phrase, 'because it is in contradiction to the view of emptiness' in the *Commentary on Logic*.
- The followers of Mind Only use the term *emptiness* for the emptiness of any substantial difference between subject and object. This is expressed by the phrase, 'therefore whatever is empty of duality is real'.
- We followers of the *madhyamaka* use the term 'emptiness' in two ways, first to refer to the emptiness of true existence, and second to refer to the emptiness of the elaborations that arise at the four

extremes. The first is an ordinary understanding found in all three vehicles, but the second is an extraordinary understanding specific to the *mahāyāna*.

Each of the above can be subdivided, as before, into an approximate and a definitive emptiness, but only the second subdivision of the last type of emptiness can be described as the definitive ultimate truth. Therefore in our tradition even the noble ones of the *hīnayāna* can be said to have understood the ultimate truth; however, the true nature, the realm of reality, non-elaboration and union are all free from the elaborations that arise at the four extremes, and the *hīnayāna* has not the slightest understanding of them.[23]

2.2. Path madhyamaka*: the union of the two accumulations*

This has two parts: recognizing that which is to be eliminated (the two obscurations); and recognizing the antidotes that eliminate them.

2.2.1. Recognizing that which is to be eliminated: the two obscurations

As explained earlier, the mind that fixates on the aggregates and grasps them as truly existent is grasping at the true existence of *dharmas*. It is, therefore, a cognitive obscuration. But that kind of grasping at true existence is not the only form of grasping at the true existence of *dharmas,* since the mind that grasps the other three of the four extremes is also said to be grasping at the true existence of *dharmas*. Also, the mind which breaks the solidity of grasping at true existence by apprehending things as mere labels is still said to be grasping at the true existence of *dharmas*.[24]

This grasping at the true existence of *dharmas* is the ever-present cause of grasping at the true existence of the person, and this is why it is sometimes spoken of as an affliction. In the chapter on enlightenment in the *Supreme Continuum* it is taught that afflictions in their latent state are cognitive obscurations. The commentary on *Entering the Madhyamaka* also states this, and therefore we must accept that grasping at the true existence of *dharmas* is actually a cognitive obscuration. The chapter on benefits in the *Supreme Continuum* states that the mind that conceptualizes the three spheres is also a cognitive obscuration. Putting this all together, it seems that the term 'cognitive obscuration' can refer to both manifest and latent conceptualization. The former may involve grasping at true existence or not. The latter includes latent conceptualization and latent afflictions, both of which are cognitive obscurations.[25]

In the *Supreme Continuum* there are two ways of defining obscuration by the afflictions, but they appear to be essentially the same. The works of Nāgārjuna and his disciples also seem to be in agreement. They state that grasping at the true existence of the person is the source of the fundamental and associated afflictions. Thus the obscuration by the afflictions comprises the afflictions along with their latent states. In this, Nāgārjuna and Maitreya seem to be of the same mind.

2.2.2. Recognizing the antidotes that eliminate the two obscurations

The two schools of hearers claim that emptiness that refutes a personal self based on the aggregates leads to enlightenment in all three vehicles, even if one does not understand that the aggregates lack true existence. Therefore the hearers do not accept that there is any difference in the views of the three vehicles.[26]

Those who follow Mind Only believe that those who hold the above view merely attain the enlightenment of hearers and solitary buddhas, and that to attain the enlightenment of the *mahāyāna*, one has to understand suchness, the emptiness of the duality of subject and object. Thus they accept that there is a difference between the views of the *hīnayāna* and the *mahāyāna*, but not between those of the hearers and solitary buddhas.

In the *madhyamaka* system, bringing together the positions of both Maitreya and Nāgārjuna, we say that one needs to understand the lack of self in the aggregates to attain enlightenment in any of the three vehicles. Furthermore, to attain the enlightenment of the *mahāyāna*, one has to understand the freedom from elaboration that is beyond the elaboration of the four extremes. Thus there is a very great difference between the views of the *hīnayāna* and those of the *mahāyāna*. The hearers do not understand that one should not fixate on external objects, even if only as mere labels. Since the solitary buddhas do understand this, there is a difference between the views of these two.

Thus the hearers have the power to abandon grasping at the true existence of the aggregates, but this is not problematic. Why? Because the hearers focus primarily on the person's lack of true existence rather than the aggregates' lack of true existence. Solitary buddhas on the path of seeing do focus primarily on the lack of true existence in external objects, so they do have the power to abandon grasping at true existence in external objects, but they do not have the power to abandon any other cognitive obscurations. The followers of the *mahāyāna* on the path of seeing primarily focus on freedom from the elaborations that arise at the four extremes, thus they have the power to abandon all cognitive obscurations. That is the essential point.[27]

The fact that the hearers and solitary buddhas can understand lack of true existence has been explained many times in the works of Nāgārjuna and his disciples. And the *Ornament of Realization* contains many discussions of the different views found in the *hīnayāna* and the *mahāyāna*; yet it does not make a distinction between whether or not they understand lack of self. So it is clear that these two traditions are in agreement.

— 'The *Ornament of Realization* states that there is a difference between *hīnayāna* and *mahāyāna* based on whether or not one apprehends things as *dharmas*. So this difference also applies to understanding the lack of true existence.'

Not necessarily. In the *hīnayāna, dharmas* are apprehended as mere labels, which means that its followers understand lack of true existence but not the unelaborated nature of any *dharma*.

Now, the unparalleled lord of the *dharma* has said that the hearers and solitary buddhas do not understand the lack of true existence in the aggregates, citing this scriptural passage as proof:[28]

> Seeing that the three realms always lack self and substance,
> And are not autonomous agents,
> They meditate to accustom themselves to this,
> And are liberated from all transmigrations.

However, even he must accept that this passage actually seems to show that they *do* understand the lack of true existence. The passage explains that they understand that the three realms lack substance, and he has said to me that the concepts involved in grasping at substance are the same as those that grasp at true existence.

In brief, the main thing that the hearers understand is the lack of personal self, but to understand this they need to negate grasping the aggregates as truly existent. This is because grasping the aggregates as truly existent is the powerful and ever-present cause of grasping at a personal self. The main thing that the solitary buddhas understand is the lack of true existence in external objects. The main thing that the followers of the *mahāyāna* understand is freedom from the elaboration of the four extremes resulting from dualistic apprehension. Thus there is a very great difference between these views.

— 'This contradicts the *Ten Stages Sutra,* which states that bodhisattvas cannot surpass the mental faculties of the hearers and solitary buddhas before they reach the seventh stage.'

The meaning of this seems to accord with what we are teaching, as it goes on to say:

> A bodhisattva abiding on the seventh bodhisattva stage utterly transcends the activities of the hearers and solitary buddhas because he also abides in the greatness of understanding his own subject.

The meaning of this passage is as follows. 'His own subject' is the subject which is specific to the *mahāyāna* and not found in the *hīnayāna,* the same freedom from elaboration that was explained earlier. Some understanding of it as a general idea is also present in the *mahāyāna* paths of accumulation and application. The superiority of this approach to the hearers and solitary buddhas is explained in the section of the *Ornament of Realization* on ending the apprehension of true existence. Direct awareness of the freedom from elaborations exists on the *mahāyāna* path of seeing, and the superiority of this approach is explained in the section stating, 'because their path surpasses all others, it is the superior path'.

The word 'greatness' refers to the power to negate all grasping at characteristics. This approach surpasses the hearers and solitary buddhas when one reaches the seventh stage, and from the eighth stage upwards, grasping at characteristics cannot manifest at all. So, if we understand the power of the five phrases: 'his own subject', 'understanding it', 'its greatness', 'also', and 'utterly', this passage cannot serve as a basis for the mistaken idea that there is no difference between the views of the *hīnayāna* and *mahāyāna*.

I think that the *Perfection of Wisdom Sutra*, the *Ten Stages Sutra*, the *Ornament of Realization* and the words of Nāgārjuna make the same point, but when it is necessary they use terminology in slightly different ways. The *Ornament of Realization* is mainly concerned with the path of the extraordinary *mahāyāna*. Therefore it defines the understanding of non-elaboration as the lack of self in *dharmas*, and says that the hearers and solitary buddhas do not have it. On the other hand, the supreme Nāgārjuna writes that all three vehicles understand non-arising, and since he also defines the lack of self in *dharmas* in terms of non-arising, he is saying that this is present in all three vehicles.

2.3. Result madhyamaka*: the union of the two buddha bodies*

This is explained extensively elsewhere.[29]

3. Relating the above to the scriptures to inspire confidence

Though I ought to relate every part of this brief presentation of our system to texts that can be taken as proof, I fear that would be excessive here. So rather than elaborating, I will only do what is necessary, relating the following two points to scriptural texts: the division of the ultimate truth into categorizable and uncategorizable; and freedom from the elaborations of the four extremes.

3.1. The division of the ultimate truth into categorizable and uncategorizable

From the Indian master Jñānagarbha:

> The refutation of arising and the rest is indeed valid, as shown by the arguments refuting the validity of entities that are conceptualized as arising and so on. We say that this is an ultimate truth. Yet others grasp it as the only thing that is valid, and this is why we say, 'and the rest'. When analyzed, it also turns out to be just a convention. Why is that? If the object negated does not exist, then it is clear that the negation cannot validly exist either.

Śāntarakṣita states:

> We have previously classified non-arising and the rest as valid conventions. However, we also call them 'ultimate' because they accord with the ultimate. They liberate us from all of the elaborations that conceptualize things as valid. The actual ultimate abandons the entire net of elaborations including *dharma* and non-*dharma*, arising and non-arising, empty and non-empty. We call non-arising and the rest 'ultimate' in an approximate way because they help to enter that state.

Also, Candrakīrti says in his commentary on the *Sixty Reasons*, 'We posit the two truths based on the minds of ordinary people.' Others, including Dragpa Gyaltsen, Chegom Sherab Dorje, and the learned Rendawa, seem to make the same point.

3.2. *Freedom from the elaborations of the four extremes*

I won't write here about all of the many statements in Nāgārjuna's philosophical and devotional works. The *Entrance to the Two Truths* states:

> Prince, on the ultimate level, if the ultimate truth itself were by nature an object of body, speech, or mind, it would not be what we understand as 'ultimate truth.' It would in fact be a conventional truth. On the contrary, prince, on the ultimate level the ultimate is beyond all terminology. It is without divisions, not arising or ceasing, free from speech and that which is spoken of, free from knowledge and that which is known. Prince, the ultimate truth transcends even being an object of those perfect omniscient ones. Nor is it expressed in the phrase, 'ultimate truth.'

The *Sutra of the Questions of Kaśyapa* states:

> Kaśyapa, a view of the personal self that is larger than Mount Meru would be better than an arrogant person's view of emptiness. Why is that? As I have explained elsewhere, emptiness eliminates all philosophical views, but it is impossible to cure those who take emptiness itself as a view.

The *Perfection of Wisdom in Twenty-Five Thousand Lines* states:

> Those who become attached to the emptiness of form and stay with that, or become attached to the emptiness of feeling, perception, motivation, or consciousness and stay there, are desperate for a *dharma* that approximates that of a bodhisattva, a great being. This is a fault.

And the *Perfection of Wisdom in One Hundred Thousand Lines* states:

> Even what we call emptiness is not established. Do not apprehend even emptiness.

The *Sutra of the Questions of the Bodhisattva Aśvaghoṣa* shows that apprehending the nonexistence of conventions is not the same as nihilism:

> Bhagavān, if everything is empty, does this result in nihilism? The Bhagavān said, 'Noble child, a nihilist view is identified as such based on three characteristics: denying that the causes and effects of actions exist as conventions; being attached exclusively to the extreme of nonexistence; and being attached to the word "emptiness" without understanding the meaning of the profound *dharma*.'

Thus the essential point is this. The followers of the *madhyamaka* have specific *madhyamaka* paths for abandoning the dualistic extremes that occur in all of the three vehicles. The followers of the *hīnayāna* need to be liberated from the extreme of eternalism by the fact that ultimately nothing is established, and they need to be liberated from the extreme of nihilism by the fact that, conventionally, the causes and effects of actions are not belittled. This was taught in the *Jewel Garland*.

Based on this, the *mahāyāna* teaches three things: (i) a special view that is free from all dualistic grasping at the essence of reality, like ideas of existence and nonexistence; (ii) compassion directed towards sentient beings; and (iii) the generation of the awakening mind of the *mahāyāna*. Having combined these together, we meditate, and thereby attain the final result. At that time, without moving from the state of freedom from elaboration in the realm of reality, one spontaneously and effortlessly brings benefit to sentient beings throughout space.

CHAPTER SIX

THE PATH

Introduction to the Tantras

The practices of the vajrayāna *play a central role in Tibetan Buddhism and their centrality is one of the principal ways the Buddhism that developed in Tibet differs from those traditions now practised in East and Southeast Asia. Aspects of Tibetan Buddhism that make it visibly distinct – for example, initiation ceremonies, wrathful deities, ritual accoutrements such as the* vajra *and bell – are not 'Tibetan' as such but are the practices and material culture of the* vajrayāna. *The text translated here, by the twelfth-century scholar Sonam Tsemo, explains the nature of the* vajrayāna *and how it differs from, yet is compatible with, other forms of Buddhist practice.*

Vajrayāna is often called 'tantric Buddhism', a name that is accurate in that the practices of the *vajrayāna* are drawn from Buddhist scriptures known as 'tantras'. The tantras, which first began to circulate in India in the sixth or seventh centuries BCE, can be distinguished from the *sūtras* by the practices they teach, though both are considered to be the words of the Buddha. In the tantras we find practices not present in the *sūtras,* involving the visualization *maṇḍalas* of deities representing different aspects of enlightenment and the recitation of mantras. Tantra (*rgyud* in Tibetan) means 'continuity' and the basic principle of tantric practice is the continuity between the state of an ordinary sentient being and that of a buddha. Despite these differences, the basic concepts and aspirations of the tantras overlap with the *sūtras,* and for this reason Tibetan Buddhists consider the *vajrayāna* to be an extension of the *mahāyāna,* differing mainly in the practices taught.

In *mahāyāna* Buddhism, the Buddha Śākyamuni is one of many buddhas, specifically the one who manifested in physical form (*nirmāṇakāya*) in this world, and in this age. Other buddhas, such as Amitābha, exist in other realms, where they cannot be directly perceived, but are accessible through devotion. In addition, there are bodhisattvas representing specific qualities and activities of an enlightened buddha; for example, Mañjuśrī, embodying enlightened wisdom and knowledge, and Avalokiteśvara, embodying enlightened compassion.

The practices of the *vajrayāna* create a relationship between the practitioner and a buddha or bodhisattva. The nature of the relationship depends on the kind of tantric practice. In some practices it may be a relationship of devotion to an external power; in others, the practitioner takes on the identity of the deity, recognizing in themselves the enlightened qualities of that buddha or bodhisattva. In either case, the goal is the transformation of the practitioner.

The great variety of practices presented in the tantras led to various systems of classification. The one presented in the text translated here came to be used by most schools of Tibetan Buddhism. This system enumerates four classes of tantra: the two lower classes of *kriyā* and *carya*; and the two higher classes of yoga and supreme yoga. The lower classes of tantra are distinguished from the higher in that they concentrate on practices that lead to 'ordinary accomplishments' that support the practitioner but do not lead to enlightenment; the higher classes of tantra, on the other hand, concentrate on practices leading to enlightenment, the 'supreme accomplishment'.

The four classes of tantra also differ in terms of their emphasis on external ritual activity as against internal methods of visualization. The *kriyā* (meaning 'action') tantras teach primarily external rituals; the *carya* (meaning 'conduct') tantras teach a combination of external and internal practices; the yoga tantras mainly teach meditation; and the supreme yoga tantras teach especially advanced meditation practices.[1]

It is these advanced meditation practices, which may also involve sexual and violent imagery, that have been the most open to misinterpretation and misuse. The interpretation of these practices by Indian and Tibetan masters has emphasized their context in the *mahāyāna* Buddhist aspiration to achieve buddhahood for all living beings. The sometimes shocking imagery also illustrates an important point about the *vajrayāna*, made in the text translated here, that its method is to accept and transform emotions such as desire and hatred into their inherent enlightened aspects.

Tibetan Buddhist practices such as those we have looked at in the previous chapters, which are based on the *sūtras* rather than the tantras, require the practitioner to renounce the objects of desire that cause mental anguish. In addition, they rely on the use of contemplations, such as considering death and impermanence, as 'antidotes' to negative mental states. The approach in tantric practices is different: one's emotional reactions to things are directly transformed, so there is no need to renounce the objects that provoke those reactions.

In this transformation, the 'five poisons' become five aspects of wisdom: desire becomes the wisdom of discernment; anger becomes the mirror-like wisdom; ignorance becomes the wisdom of reality itself; pride becomes the wisdom of equality; and jealousy becomes the all-accomplishing wisdom. Another way of understanding this is that nothing needs to be transformed: the practice of *vajrayāna* simply allows the inherent enlightened qualities of these negative emotional states to become naturally manifest.

The practice of *vajrayāna*

The practice of *vajrayāna* begins with the *mahāyāna* practices described in previous chapters. The transition from these practices to the *vajrayāna* involves an initiation ceremony, as Sonam Tsemo writes:

> To begin with, while developing the awakening mind, one practises in a similar way to the path of the perfections. Then, when it is time to enter the *maṇḍala* and perform the empowerment, the master blesses the body, speech, and mind of the student as the *vajra* body,

> speech, and mind of the buddhas. Next, while remaining inseparable from that experience, one meditates on the two stages of the path.

Thus the practice of *vajrayāna* takes the form of initiation ceremonies, the regular daily practice of recitation and visualization known as *sādhana,* and a continuing commitment to a special set of vows known as *samaya.* The regular practice of *sādhana* is usually performed alone, but regular group recitation practices are undertaken as well. We will look at these communal practices in the following chapter, focussing here on how initiation is connected with individual meditation practice.

The initiation ceremony is the entry gate to *vajrayāna* meditation practice, and it is generally held that practising without having previously received the relevant initiation is at best ineffective, at worst harmful. The student receives an initiation from the teacher and the deity as a non-duality; the teacher represents the deity and the deity is immanent in the teacher. In the course of initiation, the deity becomes immanent in the student as well, and this is the basis for all subsequent meditation practice focussed on that deity.

There are several different forms of initiation depending on the level of tantric practice being undertaken. The more elaborate ceremony, usually intended for practices of the tantras of yoga and supreme yoga, is empowerment (Skt. *abhiṣeka,* Tib. *dbang*). Those who receive an empowerment become identical with the deity that they are to practice, through the agency of the lama, who is qualified through his or her own practice of the deity. This identification with the deity is the basis for subsequent *sādhana* practice.

The simpler form of initiation, which is used for most practices from the lower tantras, involves being granted a blessing or receiving a permission. These usually establish a relationship, rather than identification, with the deity. In all initiations, a textual transmission (*lung*) and meditation instruction (*khrid*) is also required in order to practise the associated recitation and visualization. The vows associated with these initiations are different as well. The full initiations of the higher tantras entail a commitment to the special *vajrayāna* vows known as the vows of the *vidyādhara*.

These vows are enumerated in different ways in different tantric lineages, but the fundamental vow in all traditions is the vow not to think ill of the lama. This is because in the ceremony of empowerment the lama is the connection between the student and the deity who is the focus of their meditation practice. In the empowerment ceremony and afterwards, the lama represents the enlightened state of all the buddhas, and it is through recognizing this in the lama that the students can come to recognize it in themselves.[2]

In *sādhana* practice, the practioner sits and visualizes the deity, either in front of or above them, as an object of devotion, or as their own body. The outer environment is also visualized as the palace of the *maṇḍala*, situated in a pure realm. To avoid attachment to the visualization itself, the meditation instructions usually emphasize that these forms are empty and should be experienced as luminous but insubstantial. Neverthless, the forms of some of the deities may be visualized in great detail, down to the details of their jewellery. Some deities have many heads or arms, with hands holding a variety of objects, and these always have symbolic significance. At the same time as visualizing the deity, the practitioner recites the deity's specific mantra (for example, the well-known mantra, *oṃ maṇi padme hūṃ*, is the mantra of Avalokiteśvara).[3] In some practices, physical gestures known as *mūdra* are also employed, which, along with visualization and recitation, bring the practitioner's body, speech, and mind into the practice.

The practice of deity yoga itself is divided into two stages: the stage of development; and the stage of completion. In the development stage the practitioner cultivates the identification of his or herself with the deity through recitation and visualization. In the completion stage, which generally comes after the accomplishment of the development stage, the focus of meditation is on the body's internal energies and channels. As Sonam Tsemo explains in the text translated here, these practices lead to a transformation of perception. The ordinary conceptual grasping at things as pleasant, unpleasant, or neutral, gradually disappears, revealing what Sonam Tsemo describes as 'the vast extent of joys'.

Though a practitioner may receive many empowerments, permissions, and blessings, he or she would normally only engage in the regular practice of a few of them, following the guidance of a lama. The regular practice of *sādhana* is structured in much the same way as other practices in Tibetan Buddhism, beginning with the brief prayers of taking refuge in the three jewels and generating the aspiration to bring all sentient beings to buddhahood. The main part of the practice involving visualization and recitation of mantras follows. At the end, the recitation stops, the visualization is dissolved, and the practitioner rests in a quiet period of 'just sitting'.

Vajrayāna in Tibet

It is in terms of the *vajrayāna* that the historical distinction between the two phases of the transmission of Buddhism into Tibet makes most sense. It was the tantric transmissions of the first period (eighth–ninth centuries CE) that formed the basis of the Nyingma school, also known as the school of the early translations. The Tibetan emperors supported the translation of tantras as well as *sūtras*, which were always undertaken by a team that included at least one Indian translator. However, the highest-level tantras, known at that time as *mahāyoga*, were kept out of general circulation. After the collapse of the Tibetan empire, tantric practices spread throughout Tibet. This widespread practice of *vajrayāna*, combined with the paucity of Indian teachers who could provide authoritative guidance, prompted the invitation to Atiśa and other Indian masters to come and teach in Tibet.

The later transmission of Buddhism into Tibet was, unlike the first transmission, mainly concerned with tantric texts, and involved Tibetans travelling to Nepal and India, and teachers from those countries visiting Tibet. Due to changes in the tantric lineages popular in India at that time, many tantras that had not previously been translated were introduced into Tibet, along with new systems of interpretation based upon them. Among the practice lineages that appeared in

Tibet at this time, the Sakya and Kagyu schools have been the most enduring. Among the new schools, the Sakyas were the only ones to maintain a connection to the 'old' practices (such as the deity Vajrakīlaya) alongside their new tantric lineages.

The founder of Sakya, Khon Konchog Gyalpo (1034–1102), was the first of his family to study the new tantric lineages, which included the *Guhyasamāja, Cakrasaṃvara,* and *Hevajra* tantras. These studies were continued by his son, Sachen Kunga Nyingpo, who also specialized in the practices known as *lamdre,* 'the path that incorporates the result'. Sachen's two sons, Sonam Tsemo and Dragpa Gyaltsen, wrote some of the defining works of Tibetan *vajrayāna,* including the latter's *Dispelling Error,* on the tantric vows, and the former's *Introduction to the Tantras,* part of which is translated here.

Introducing the Tantras

At the beginning of his work, Sonam Tsemo places the *vajrayāna* within the context of the Buddhist path in general. The three chapters translated here are *The Essence of the Path, The Divisions of the Path,* and *The Characteristics of Each Division.* Sonam Tsemo's aim is to show that the *vajrayāna* is not a separate vehicle ranked above the *mahāyāna,* rather it is part of the *mahāyāna,* distinguished mainly by the efficacy of its practices. The *mahāyāna,* in turn, builds on the basic teachings shared by all Buddhist schools.

It may be useful to think of Sonam Tsemo as sketching a map for the great variety of Buddhist practices that were coming into Tibet in his time. So, in the first chapter, 'the essentials of the path' is about the Buddhist path in general. Sonam Tsemo explains several aspects of the Buddhist path that distinguish it from other ways of life, including taking refuge in the three jewels (the Buddha, the *dharma,* and the *sangha*) and accepting the four 'seals', or characteristics, of existence:

- All composite things are impermanent.
- All contaminated things are imbued with suffering.

- All *nirvāṇa* is peace and bliss.
- All entities are without self.

Taking refuge and accepting these four seals makes one a Buddhist, though, as Sonam Tsemo points out, one could be a Buddhist without accepting the four seals, as shown by the existence of the Personalist school. Those who follow the *mahāyāna* are said to go beyond these basic teachings in the extent of their compassion and wisdom. The 'great compassion' of the *mahāyāna* is represented by the bodhisattva vow to achieve liberation for all sentient beings; the 'great wisdom' is the true understanding of emptiness represented by the *madhyamaka*.

What kind of realization is achieved by those Buddhists who do not follow the *mahāyāna*? Sonam Tsemo explores various answers to this question given by previous Buddhist scholars before settling on 'three paths with one result', meaning that the paths of hearers, solitary buddhas, and bodhisattvas all lead to the same kind of enlightenment. The hearers and solitary buddhas first achieve a state of peace that they think is enlightenment, but that is really a temporary insensate state; once they awake from this, they attain the full enlightenment of a buddha.

So, according to Sonam Tsemo, the *mahāyāna* builds upon elements that are found in the *hīnayāna,* taking them further in the extent of its great compassion and wisdom; hence the name 'the greater vehicle'. This understanding of the relationship between the *hīnayāna* and the *mahāyāna* was accepted by almost all Tibetan Buddhists. On the other hand, the relationship between the *mahāyāna* and the *vajrayāna* is more controversial.

Rather than distinguishing *mahāyāna* from *vajrayāna,* Sonam Tsemo prefers to speak of the difference between the practices of the perfections (*pāramitā*) and the practice of the secret mantra (*guhyamantra*). This is significant in that it makes the distinction about practice, rather than philosophy or aspiration, and thus the great compassion and wisdom of the *mahāyāna* are taken as the basis of the *vajrayāna* as well. To put it another way, the *vajrayāna* is a specific aspect of the *mahāyāna,* distinguished by its practices.

For Sonam Tsemo, the most fundamental difference between the two methods is between the practice of rejection and the practice of acceptance. What is rejected or accepted? The five 'objects of desire' are the objects of the five senses: sight, hearing, touch, taste, and smell. In the practices of the perfections, these five are considered the basis of *saṃsāra*, and are to be renounced. In the practice of the secret mantra, on the other hand, the basis is not to be abandoned. Here, the five objects of desire actually act as the basis for liberation. Sonam Tsemo explains how this can be:

> The objects do not bring about enslavement through their own essence. It is the erroneous concepts based on those objects that bring about enslavement. When these, the real causes of enslavement, are abandoned, then the objects that have been the causes of enslavement become the causes of liberation.

Thus it is not the objects of the senses that are the problem, but the way we conceive of them. In Sonam Tsemo's words, we conceive of them as 'ordinary' (*tha mal*), meaning that we respond to them with our ordinary reactions of desire, aversion, or indifference. The practices of the secret mantra, the development and completion stages of meditation, overturn this conceptualization of the objects of our senses in the ordinary way. In a state of non-conceptualization, they are all experienced as joyful.

Though the end result of these practices is the same as that achieved by those who only undertake the practices of the perfections, it is said to be achieved much more quickly. This is one reason the *vajrayāna* is also known as 'the vehicle of the result'. Another reason, as explained by Sonam Tsemo at the end of the text translated here, is that the *vajrayāna* takes the result – the state of being a buddha – as the basis for the practices themselves.

INTRODUCTION TO THE TANTRAS

The essentials of the path

This comprises two parts: the definition of the path, and its subdivisions.

1. Definition

The 'path' is the method for achieving the result that is aimed at by an individual.

2. Subdivisions

This is in two parts: the ordinary and extraordinary paths.

2.1. The ordinary paths

There are three types: first, paths that lead to birth in the lower realms, including certain people such as the inferior non-Buddhists who hold nihilistic views; second, paths that lead to the attainment of the happy realms, including the superior non-Buddhists, such as the Jains; and third, paths that lead to the attainment of liberation – the paths of the hearers and solitary buddhas.

2.2. The extraordinary path

This is presented in two parts: the reason for teaching the ordinary paths; and the presentation of the extraordinary *mahāyāna*.

2.2.1. The reason for teaching the ordinary paths

Since the extraordinary path is entirely sufficient, what is achieved by teaching the ordinary paths? There are three things it achieves:

First, it enables the followers of the *mahāyāna* to guide various types of sentient being. The *Supreme Continuum* says that there are three types of sentient being: those who desire worldly existence; those who renounce desire for worldly existence; and those who have no desire for either of the above.

What does this mean? The ones who desire worldly existence are the inferior non-Buddhists. As for those who desire peace, there are two types: the ones who don't know the methods, and those who do. The former are the superior non-Buddhists, and the latter are the hearers and solitary buddhas. The third type, who consider both worldly existence and peace to be equal, are the bodhisattvas. This is expressed in *The Way of the Bodhisattva*: 'Liberated from the extremes of attachment and destruction, they work while remaining in *saṃsāra*.'

Therefore, it is necessary to teach each of these three types their own path, and once they have practised it, to guide them to the *mahāyāna*. As it says in the *Sutra of Unravelling the Knot*: 'There is nobody whom the conqueror's children will not instruct.'

Second, the ordinary paths are taught to clear away doubts about the path by understanding what conforms with it and what does not. Through understanding all paths, one can distinguish the particular features of each. This is important because we abandon inclinations towards other paths by understanding the superiority of our own.

Third, the ordinary paths are taught to counteract the pride of those who follow the *mahāyāna* when even these ordinary paths have not yet arisen in their mindstreams. Such people, who have not even developed the attitude of a superior non-Buddhist, declare, 'I am a follower of the *mahāyāna*.' It is important for them to distinguish between their own path and those of others in order to understand the real meaning of the *mahāyāna*.

2.2.2. The presentation of the extraordinary mahāyāna

Those are the reasons we teach the ordinary paths. Now, the definition of the *mahāyāna*, which is the extraordinary path, is in three parts: the essence of the extraordinary path; the ways in which it is superior to the ordinary paths; and different interpretations of this superiority.

2.2.2.1. Essence

The *mahāyāna* is the method for attaining the result, omniscience itself.

2.2.2.2. The ways in which it is superior to the ordinary paths

There are four ways in which the *mahāyāna* is superior to the ordinary paths: because we practise the methods for abolishing suffering; because we have no desire for *saṃsāra*; because we practise the methods for liberation, the vehicle for buddhahood; and, finally, because we do not desire this liberation alone, but practise the *mahāyāna*. On this path, *saṃsāra* and *nirvāṇa* we one and the same, and we teach that this is equivalent to the non-duality of compassion and emptiness.

2.2.2.2.1. Practising the methods for abolishing suffering

This has two aspects. First, abolishing suffering of this life. Because we practise the teachings from the traditional sources, we are superior to the confused ones, such as cowherds, who do not follow any school. Second, abolishing the suffering of future lives. Because we believe in the causes and effects of our actions, the path to the higher realms has appeared in our minds. Therefore we are superior to unwholesome schools which hold mistaken views, such as the Hedonists.

2.2.2.2.2. Having no desire for saṃsāra

We think, 'Alas! Even if I want to abolish suffering, I won't be liberated from suffering if I don't abandon this samsaric existence. Only by doing so will I attain liberation.' This is the attitude by which we abandon all worldly paths. The same attitude exists to some extent among superior non-Buddhists, but they do not practise genuine methods for liberation.

2.2.2.2.3. Practising the methods for liberation, the vehicle for buddhahood

This has two aspects. The first is holding the three jewels as our refuge. Once we have taken refuge in the Buddha, we abandon the desire for worldly teachers, such as Śiva, and their state of being. Once we have taken refuge in the *dharma*, we practise it by abandoning worldly paths based on harming sentient beings. Once we have taken refuge in the *sangha*, we abandon companions who follow non-Buddhist teachings.

The second aspect is accepting the view of the four seals. By the very fact of having sought refuge, we have accepted the four seals:

- All composite things are impermanent.
- All contaminated things are imbued with suffering.
- All *nirvāṇa* is peace and bliss.
- All entities are without self.

On the other hand, if one holds the three jewels as a refuge, one is a Buddhist even if one has not accepted the four seals. The Personalists are an example of this. Some say that the Bhagavān has stated that these people are not Buddhists. If that were the case, then consider this statement from the *Perfection of Wisdom Sutra*: 'Those who do not say that all phenomena are without essence are not my students.' This would mean that even the followers of the Mind Only school would suffer the same consequence.

The above reasons show how the *mahāyāna* is superior to all non-Buddhist schools.

2.2.2.2.4. Practising the mahāyāna *in which the path of the equality of worldly existence and quiescence is taught to be the non-duality of compassion and emptiness*

Those who practise the *mahāyāna* in particular are superior to those who do not practise any system because they engage in abolishing suffering in the ways shown earlier. They are superior to non-Buddhists because they hold to the three jewels. They are superior to the hearers and solitary buddhas because they practise equanimity towards worldly existence and quiescence.

What are the specific ways in which they are superior to the hearers? I will answer this question in three parts: first, distinguishing the *mahāyāna* and the *hīnayāna* in terms of their scriptural collections and philosophical systems; second, defining the *mahāyāna* and the *hīnayāna* in terms of the path and its result, and third, giving the reason for defining them in terms of both scriptural collections and the path and result.

2.2.2.2.4.1. Distinguishing the mahāyāna *and the* hīnayāna *in terms of their scriptural collections and philosophical systems*

The twelve branches of scripture that are held by the proud hearers, such as the seven *abhidharma* treatises, are what we refer to as the scriptural collections of the hearers. The vastly extensive scriptural collection, which includes the *Perfection of Wisdom* and *Flower Garland Sutra,* which we refer to as the scriptural collections of the *mahāyāna,* is unknown to them. Careful examination of those two texts alone shows that they contain limitless features. Nevertheless, the noble *Mission to Lanka Sutra* summarizes the *mahāyāna* as follows:

> In the five topics and the three natures,
> In the eight kinds of consciousness,
> And the reality of the two kinds of non-self,
> The whole of the *mahāyāna* is contained.

The five topics are: names, causal factors, concepts, thusness, and genuine wisdom. The three natures are the labelled, dependent, and thoroughly established levels of truth. The eight consciousnesses are the six senses (that is, sight and the rest), the ego, and the base consciousness. The two non-selves are the lack of self in the person and in entities. These teachings characterize the texts of the *mahāyāna.* Extensive discussions of this can be found elsewhere in the works of teachers such as Nāgārjuna and Asaṅga.

2.2.2.2.4.2. Defining the mahāyāna *and the* hīnayāna *in terms of the path and its result*

The *Ornament of the Sutras* states:

> The great vision itself,
> And along with that, the two accomplishments,
> Striving diligently towards wisdom,
> Using skill in means,
> The great genuine accomplishment,
> And the vast activities of Buddhahood –
> Because it is endowed with these seven greatnesses
> We call it the great vehicle.

The first five of these are the means by which the vehicle moves. They are the path. The last two are the place to which the vehicle goes. They are the result, the great benefit for oneself and others. Several methods for establishing this difference have been taught, but these seven should be understood as condensing them all. They can be further condensed into the pair of great compassion and great wisdom. Thus the *mahāyāna* is superior in terms of its scriptures and its path and result.

2.2.2.2.4.3. The reason for defining the mahāyāna *and the* hīnayāna *in terms of scriptural collections as well as in terms of path and result*

Some people might think, 'If it is appropriate to explain the scriptural collections and philosophical systems when distinguishing these two, what is the point of explaining the path and its result? And vice versa if one explains the path and its result.' This is wrong. Those who follow the school of the hearers say that the real *mahāyāna* is the scriptural collections that they understand, while others, such as the *Perfection of Wisdom,* were not spoken by the Buddha. It is to refute this that the scriptural collections and philosophical systems are distinguished. This is also intended to establish that the *mahāyāna* is the word of the Buddha.

Furthermore, some people who follow the *mahāyāna* have the mistaken belief that they could never be hearers or solitary buddhas because they have read *mahāyāna* scriptures. It is to clear up this misconception that we show the features of the path and its result. Even those who adhere to the philosophical systems of the *mahāyāna* will become hearers if their minds do not contain the seven greatnesses.

2.2.2.3. *Different interpretations of this superiority*

There are four different interpretations.

First, three paths with three results. This is maintained by the master Asaṅga and others. They teach that the scriptural collections of the hearers bring about the attainment of the state of an *arhat* or solitary buddha, while the scriptural collections of the *mahāyāna* bring about the attainment of the state of a buddha. Even here, those who stray from the path become hearers or solitary buddhas. Thus the *mahāyāna* includes the paths of the three types.

Second, one path with three results. The master Candrakīrti considers that the philosophical systems of the hearers do not even lead to the attainment of the state of an *arhat*. The three types can all be liberated by the philosophical system of the *mahāyāna*, whereas the only purpose of the philosophical system of the hearers is to lead to the *mahāyāna*.

Third, one path with one result. Some people maintain that when one follows the *mahāyāna* path, individual liberation is temporarily accomplished before final buddhahood.

Fourth, three paths with one result. This is maintained by some masters based on the *Lotus Sutra* and the like. As shown by the example of the householder, people are temporarily situated on the three paths until they finally awaken to buddhahood. As it says in the *Mission to Lanka*:

Once they have attained a meditational body,
They do not awaken for eons,
But this is like intoxication or a swoon.

Once this is gone, they attain my body,
That which is known as the *buddhadharma*.

This interpretation is essentially the same assertion that there is one path and one result. Therefore I agree with both of these. The first two interpretations can be shown, through scripture and reasoning, to be provisional teachings. All of these above interpretations are extensively explained in scriptures such as the *Sixty Reasons*, the *Jewel Garland*, the *Supreme Continuum*, and the *Awakening of Vairocana*, and can best be understood there.

Although my venerable lama did not teach the definition of the essential nature of the path in this context, I have taken his teachings from elsewhere and written them down here because it was necessary. Why was it necessary? If one tries to classify the path without knowing its general features, there will be no basis for classification, and the system of classification will be awkward.

Both the perfections and the secret mantra are the *mahāyāna*, and when people do not know the basic features of the *mahāyāna*, their understanding becomes flawed. In this land of snows one sees certain practitioners of secret mantra who say that the *mahāyāna* itself is unintelligent, and certain hearers calling themselves followers of the *mahāyāna* who say that the texts of the secret mantra are depraved. I have spoken of the basis for classification here in order to purify those who hold these mistaken views.

The divisions of the path

This is in four parts: the basis for the divisions; the significance of the divisions; identifying their number; and the significance of their names.

1. The basis for the divisions

As I have shown above, the *mahāyāna* is classified according to the textual traditions, and according to the path and its result. This is the basis for classification.

2. The significance of the divisions

There are two divisions: the *mahāyāna* of the perfections (*pāramitā*) and the *mahāyāna* of the secret mantra (*guhyamantra*). The *mahāyāna* scriptures that do not contain the four superiorities are known as the vehicle of the perfections, while those scriptures that are ennobled with the four superiorities are known as the vehicle of the secret mantra.[4] These two paths are not, however, mutually exclusive or incompatible with each other. This is a distinction between the general and the specific, or between that which is superior and that which is not. This is because that which is general, the vehicle of perfections, serves as the ordinary path in both. The specific path is the *vajrayāna*, which is superior due to its depth and extent. The differences between these two will be explained in detail below. This is the significance of the divisions.

3. Identifying their number

As we have seen, the number of the divisions is two. This section also contains two parts: the twofold path, and the twofold result. Both of these will be explained by means of reasoning and scripture.

3.1. The twofold path

This is how we use reason to show that the path is twofold. In general, all *dharma* teachings have been spoken for practitioners, and there are two types of practitioner. Some people have few afflictions in general, and little craving for the objects of desire in particular, and they wish to attain enlightenment by abandoning them. The vehicle of the perfections was taught with their dull sense faculties in mind. Other people have many afflictions in general, and great craving for the objects of desire in particular, yet they wish to attain unsurpassable enlightenment. The vehicle of secret mantra was taught with their sharp sense faculties in mind.

— 'If the secret mantra is taught for those who have more afflictions, then since those with more afflictions are inferior, how can the secret mantra be superior?'

In fact, having more afflictions does not make a person inferior. Being unable to resort to antidotes is what makes them inferior. Because it conquers these stronger afflictions, the secret mantra is a more powerful method. As it says in the *Ornament of the Sutras*:

> For those who possess these powerful methods,
> The afflictions become aspects of enlightenment.
> Since their very being pacifies *saṃsāra,*
> The conqueror's children are inconceivable.

Take this metaphor: If you only have a small flame (the antidote) you cannot use it to set light to a large pile of wood (that which is to be abandoned); but if you have a bigger flame, the wood itself helps to create a huge blaze.

A possible objection is that the perfections and secret mantra also identify methods for people of three levels: greater, middling, and lesser. But different kinds of division can exist without contradiction, and here we are identifying the path as twofold based on the division of people into two types.

Now to establish this with scripture. In the *Kiss Tantra,* the Bhagavān taught the following:

> The *mahāyāna* is the bodhisattva path and its result. Therefore it was established in the *sūtras* of the perfections so that the seven greatnesses might be put into practice. The *vajrayāna* is superior because it is better than them. Since it brings about accomplishments such as achieving buddhahood in this life, its results are the sublime qualities.

Furthermore, the master Buddhaguhya taught the following in his précis of the *Awakening of Vairocana Tantra*: 'The complete benefit of oneself and others has been taught in the sutras that explain the practices of the perfections and in those that explain the practices of the secret mantra.'

3.2. The twofold result

This is also explained through reasoning and scripture. It is a general truth that where there are differing causes, there will be different results, just as millet and rice seeds produce different plants. Thus there are two results because there are two paths. Again, from the *Kiss Tantra*:

> In this life you will attain the state of buddhahood or the state of Vajrasattva. Those who do not attain the state beyond thought go to blissfulness – this is buddhahood. But the exemplar of this state is Vajrasattva, who is perfect. Thus the result of the perfections does not accomplish everything that can be attained and everything that can be abandoned. The Vajrasattva result makes all of it manifest.

So understand that this point has been argued in many places according to both reasoning and scripture.

4. The significance of names

Consider the following phrases:

- 'Teaching the practices of the perfections and teaching the practices of the secret mantra.'
- '*Mahāyāna* and *vajrayāna*.'
- 'The scriptural collections of the bodhisattvas and the scriptural collections of the *vidyādharas*.'

They should be understood as designating a general name followed by a specific name. The general name is no more than a broad term, while the specific name refers to a particular aspect. It is like the difference between saying 'copper' and saying 'a copper pot'.

How do we know that this is the case? It has been taught in many texts, including the *Vajra Pinnacle*: 'The Teacher has said that the practices of the six perfections are mere concepts.' There are also many examples in the *Perfection of Wisdom Sutras*, such as: 'The perfection of wisdom is the secret mantra: the secret mantra of great knowledge.' So, these are the principal names.

On the other hand, there are names that identify the two paths separately:

- 'The vehicle that abandons the basis, and the vehicle that does not abandon the basis.'
- 'The vehicle of the cause and the vehicle of the result.'
- 'The ordinary and extraordinary *mahāyāna*.'

The background of these names will be explained below in the sections on each subdivision, and can be understood there. This concludes the chapter on the divisions of the path.

The characteristics of each division

Now that we know the way the path is divided, we need to understand each division clearly. Therefore I will now explain the characteristics of each in turn. I will discuss first the definition of the vehicle of the perfections, because it is the basis of the path, common to all. After that I will discuss the definition of the secret mantra, in order to show that it is superior to the vehicle of the perfections.

1. The definition of the vehicle of the perfections

This is in four parts: establishing the basis from which *saṃsāra* and *nirvāṇa* arise; explaining how abandoning the basis is the path; defining the vehicle of the perfections; and showing the time it takes to achieve the result of this path and establishing that this is the vehicle of the cause.

1.1. Establishing the basis from which saṃsāra *and* nirvāṇa *arise*

This is in two parts: showing the characteristics of the basis, and establishing that the basis is the common cause of both *saṃsāra* and *nirvāṇa*.

1.1.1. The characteristics of the basis

The term *basis* is usually defined in five parts: causes, conditions, neighbours, preliminaries, and location. Here, however, I will merely define it in terms of causes. What are these causes? When distinguished in detail, there are many, such as the aggregates, sense fields, and sense bases, but they can be summarized as the five objects of desire. You may wonder how they can be summarized as these five. Well, the creator of *saṃsāra* and *nirvāṇa* is the mind. Its objects may be also counted as six or twelve, but there is not one that does not belong to these five or derivations of them. Therefore these five are the basis.

1.1.2. The basis is the common cause of both saṃsāra *and* nirvāṇa

Is there a common basis for both *saṃsāra* and *nirvāṇa,* or are there two separate bases? There is a common basis. You might object that since those who aim for *nirvāṇa* abandon the basis, it cannot be common. It is true that there must be an abandonment, but abandonment itself requires an object, and by this reasoning it is established as the basis of *nirvāṇa* as well as *saṃsāra*. As it says in the *Treasury of Abhidharma*: 'They are the basis of sorrow, and they also contain the basis for renunciation.' And: 'They are the world, which is the source of all suffering, and the divine realms too.'

Let us begin with how the objects of desire act as the basis for *saṃsāra*. First comes the simple experience of the object. Then, due to misunderstanding its nature, there is an apprehension of 'I' and 'mine', which gives rise to attachment. Based on this, various conceptualizations occur. This sequence is known as nescience, craving, and clinging; these are the fundamental afflictions. Based on this, virtuous and non-virtuous actions are carried out, involving formations and becoming; these two are the afflictions of action. After this, sentient beings experience consciousness, names and forms, the six sense bases, contact, feeling, birth, and finally old age and death; these seven constitute suffering and are the affliction of birth.[5]

It is due to these twelve aspects of worldly existence, which are included in the three kinds of defilement, that beings cycle in *saṃsāra*. It is said in the *Extensive Play Sutra*:

> Beings, under the power of craving, becoming and nescience,
> Circle unknowingly through the five states
> Of humans, gods, and the three lower realms,
> Like the circling of a potter's wheel.

How then do the five objects of desire become the basis of *nirvāṇa*? At first there is the simple experience of the object. Then the nature of the object is understood through analysis. Thanks to this, no attachment towards the object arises, and nescience comes to a halt. Due to this, no actions are carried out, and because no actions are carried out, the affliction of birth does not occur. The subsequent stages all come to an end. As it says in *Entering the Madhyamaka*:

> When nescience comes to a halt,
> It is due to consciousness meditating on suchness.
> When both of these come to a halt,
> Neither will occur again.

Thus the objects are altered by the circumstances of one's own awareness or lack of awareness. There is no essence in the objects themselves that determines whether they become the basis for *saṃsāra* or *nirvāṇa*. This can be further illustrated with various similes. A weapon becomes powerful when placed between two enemies. When the flowers of the polygonum are eaten by a white elephant a sweet-smelling dung is produced, but when a black elephant eats them a foul-smelling dung is produced. Milk is nectar to humans but poison to snakes. When a hole is drilled in a jewel, it becomes suitable to wear as an ornament, but if it breaks, it is no longer suitable. Therefore, as it has been stated in the *Hevajra Tantra*:

In this way, within *saṃsāra,*
The jewel with five desirable qualities
Becomes poison where there is impurity
And is like nectar where there is purity.

This is the explanation of the basis.

1.2. In the vehicle of the perfections, abandoning the basis is the path

This has two aspects: regarding objects as unwholesome, and the way to abandon them.

1.2.1 Regarding objects as unwholesome

When one reflects properly on the sufferings of *saṃsāra,* one becomes disillusioned. When this disillusionment causes one to search for the origin of suffering, it is found to originate from actions. Actions cause afflictions, and afflictions develop further in dependence on objects. Therefore one comes to the conclusion that objects are the cause of suffering and develops the perception that they are unwholesome.

There are many sayings such as: 'You will never have enough objects.' And in the sutras, for example: 'The objects of desire are like poisonous leaves.' And in the *Letter to a Disciple*:

> Objects and poison are similar in that when they are first experienced they are pleasurable. Objects and poison are similar in that when they are fully ripened they are extremely unpleasant. Objects and poison are similar in that they cover you in the darkness of ignorance. Objects and poison are similar in that their power is extremely agitating and difficult to overcome.

By considering them to be unwholesome, using these and many other examples, one develops the perception that happiness consists in separating oneself from objects.

1.2.2. The correct way to abandon the basis

In the first place, terrified by *saṃsāra*, one seeks refuge in the three jewels. Then one takes the vows of moral discipline in order to practise abandonment. After that, listening to authentic scriptures and practising them with rational methods, one comes to understand the nature of objects. Subsequently, all attachment to objects is abandoned through meditation. This has two aspects: meditation at the conventional level, and meditation at the ultimate level.

1.2.2.1. Meditation at the conventional level

When desire is strongest, meditate on ugliness. When conceptualization is strongest, count the breath. When anger is strongest, meditate on loving-kindness and the like. Having done this, place the mind at rest. After that, meditate on the four kinds of mindfulness as an antidote to the four errors: purity, happiness, permanence, and grasping at self. This is an example of the teachings on this subject.

1.2.2.2. Meditation at the ultimate level

By meditating that nothing has an intrinsic nature, everything is abandoned. The conqueror has declared that desirable objects, wealth, and the whole of the three world systems are like illusions, a mirage, the moon reflected in water, or a magical emanation. This is an example of the teachings on this subject.

The above is how the way to abandon the basis is explained. Since the hearers also practise this path of abandoning the basis, how can the perfections be superior? Because the earlier paths are common to all, while the subsequent paths are specific: the vehicle of the perfections and the hearers do have the abandonment of the basis in common, but the *mahāyāna* is superior in terms of its view and activities, for the reasons I explained earlier.

1.3. Defining the path of the vehicle of the perfections

This is in two parts: defining the essential features of the path, and the way in which the realization of the path develops.

1.3.1. Defining the essential features of the path

What are the essential features of the path? There is a huge number of general definitions of the path, but they are all summarized by the six perfections. These are the activities motivated by the temporal cause of great compassion. When the activities that follow the perfection of insight are enumerated, there are said to be ten perfections in total. As it says in *Distinguishing the Middle and the Extremes*:

> Generosity, morality, patience, enthusiasm,
> Meditation, insight, means, prayer, power, and wisdom:
> These are said to be the ten perfections.

There are innumerable other classifications like these ten, as well as encapsulations such as the threefold training and the two accumulations. They can be studied in other sources.

1.3.2. The way in which the realization of the path develops

How does realization develop on this path? It is described in ten phases in the *Ornament of the Sutras*:

> Lineage, faith in the teachings,
> And after that, the development of the awakening mind,
> Accomplishing generosity and the rest,
> Practising faultlessly,
> Bringing sentient beings to full ripeness,
> Completely purifying the senses,
> *Nirvāṇa* without resting,
> Supreme enlightenment and teaching.

The same text also describes four phases:

> The attainment of the stages has four aspects:
> Faith, practising pure activities,
> The methods for realization,
> And for accomplishing the stages.

Using the names of these stages we can understand the development of the awakening mind, the perfections, and everything else I have been discussing. So first of all, the causal factor of having good fortune is known as 'lineage'. Then motivated by universal compassion, another causal factor, one takes refuge in the three jewels, resulting in 'faith in the teachings'. Next comes 'the development of the awakening mind', the basis for practising the conduct of a bodhisattva. Then come the genuine activities of the perfections ('accomplishing generosity and the rest'). These four are known as the stage achieved through faith. After that comes 'practising faultlessly' the activities of a bodhisattva, which happens when the first stage is attained. Next, 'bringing sentient beings to full ripeness' continues up to the seventh stage. After that, 'completely purifying the senses' and '*nirvāṇa* without resting' both refer to the last three stages, from which there is no return.

The above comprise the path. After the path comes the result: enlightenment, known as 'supreme enlightenment' or great *nirvāṇa*, and 'teaching', which means working for the benefit of sentient beings. This is how one proceeds via the best route towards the stage of buddhahood, by means of the six perfections. Since these activities are completely pure of the three spheres, they are called 'perfections' (literally, 'going beyond'). And it is known as a 'vehicle' because one travels by means of the path, proceeding towards the result.[6]

1.4. Showing the time it takes to achieve the result of this path

How long does it take to accomplish the result by means of this path? The best accomplish it in three incalculable eons, the middling in thirty-six, and the lesser in an inconceivable number of eons. Because the cause is extended over a long period in this way, we use the name 'causal vehicle'. It is like the way a person who has difficulty walking is called a non-walker. Certainly, activities such as serving the lama cause a variety of results, such as having wheel marks on one's hands and feet. But since these are not even similar to the ultimate result itself, they are still causes. It is like the sprout being called the cause of the barley.

Now I have said enough. The result that is accomplished by means of this path is the same one that was discussed earlier. This concludes my explanation of the ordinary vehicle through a definition of the perfections.

2. The definition of the secret mantra

This is in four parts: showing how the basis is not abandoned; defining the activities of the secret mantra; defining the *vajrayāna*; and defining it as the vehicle of the result by exploring the time it takes to accomplish that result.

2.1. How the basis is not abandoned

This is in three parts: the reason why the basis is not abandoned; how the methods of the secret mantra do not involve abandoning the basis; and the way in which one becomes free from the basis.

2.1.1. The reason why the basis is not abandoned

As I showed earlier, the basis is fivefold in that it comprises the five objects of desire. If this describes the basis and the objects from which it is comprised, how could they be abandoned? And how could those who are strongly bound to them have the strength to abandon them? In fact, it is not necessary to do so. This is explained in the *Vajra Tent*:

> Born due to desire, worldly people
> Will be liberated by desire itself.

And from the *Secret Assembly Tantra*:

> People with attachment always rely on the five objects of desire
> Because they have established that they are the five wisdoms.

But don't people become enslaved by the objects? Those who do not use the right methods will be enslaved by the objects, as ordinary people are. For those who do use the right methods, the objects themselves act as aids to liberation. This is akin to substances such as poison and fire. The objects do not bring about enslavement through their own essence. It is the erroneous concepts based on those objects that bring about enslavement. When these, the real causes of enslavement, are abandoned, then the objects that have been the causes of enslavement become the causes of liberation. The same thing is said in the glorious *Hevajra Tantra*:

> Whatever the terrible actions may be
> That have caused someone to be enslaved,
> If they possess these methods, then those same actions
> Will liberate them from the chains of existence.

2.1.2. The methods that do not abandon the basis

What then are the methods for freeing ourselves from the causes of enslavement referred to by the words 'if they possess these methods'? There are two methods that do not involve abandoning the basis: the skilful means of the development stage; and the skilful means of the completion stage.

2.1.2.1. The skilful means of the development stage

This comprises the skilful means of one's personal deity, and the skilful means of each and every deity.

2.1.2.1.1. The skilful means of one's personal deity

Every subject and object, no matter what it is, can be utilized by being understood as one's own deity. From the *Secret Assembly Tantra*:

> All enjoyment of desirable things
> Should be cultivated with whatever you desire.
> Through union with your deity,
> Offer them to yourselves and others.

This is stated elsewhere as well. This method overturns the conceptualization of ordinariness practised by those who place their faith in lesser paths.

2.1.2.1.2. The skilful means of each and every deity

Looking at the limitless extent of subjects and objects, we can understand each and every one of them as an individual deity. This is stated in the *Secret Assembly Tantra*:

> In brief, the five aggregates are the conquerors.
> All the *tathāgatas* and the sense fields too,
> Are the supreme *maṇḍala* of the bodhisattvas.

And the *Hevajra Tantra* states:

> Form is known as Gauri,
> The aspect of sound is Cauri.

And so on.[7] This destroys conceptualization that apprehends the vast extent of joys as ordinary, along with conceptualization that apprehends them as an undifferentiated whole. The cause of being enslaved is this conceptualization of ordinariness. When this ordinariness ceases in such a consciousness, then everything is gradually abandoned.

2.1.2.2. The skilful means of the completion stage

Based on whichever of the above methods one finds to be suitable, one develops a non-conceptual concentration. This changes the complexion of objects, allowing them to be enjoyed. This is also expounded in the *Later Secret Assembly Tantra*:

> By applying themselves to the completion stage,
> Which is derived from method and wisdom,
> The mantra adepts apply themselves
> To the aggregates, sense fields, sense bases, and forms.

And so on. The cause of being enslaved in this way is conceptualization. When conceptualization is cleared away by non-conceptual concentration, one is gradually liberated from all enslavement.

2.1.3. The way in which one becomes free from the basis

In general, the sole cause of enslavement is conceptualization; in particular, the conceptualization of ordinariness. Based on that, the afflictions and everything that comes from them develop stage by stage. Thus when the essential cause is cleared away by the above two methods, the complexion of the objects changes and they themselves become antidotes. This is why we should rely on the objects themselves, as in the examples given earlier. This is also stated in the *Hevajra Tantra*:

> After the poisons have been nullified by purification,
> They are themselves the supports we rely upon.

At first the antidotes are weak and one can be hurt by objects; this is known as 'appearances arising as enemies'. In the intermediate stage, when we rely on the antidotes, they are equal in strength to objects, so both harm and benefit arise at different times. This is known as 'the phase of appearances arising in different aspects'. We call these two phases 'meditative equipoise'. Finally, when the antidotes are strong, objects act as aids to realization; this state of affairs is known as 'appearances arising as guides', and is also called 'the five poisons transformed into medicine'. Because concentration is continuous, it is known as 'total meditative equipoise'. This continuous yoga is spoken of in the glorious *Kiss Tantra*:

> Each and every sensory faculty is the path itself,
> And they become the very essence of the path.
> Through yoga the lack of meditative equipoise
> Is constantly present in complete meditative equipoise.

See also lines such as, 'Viewing the variety of forms'.

2.2. Defining the activities of the secret mantra

This method, which does not abandon the basis, is known as 'the activities of the secret mantra'. What are these activities? To answer this question I will address the meaning of mantra and the activities associated with it. Elsewhere one can read extensive discussions of the original source of mantras, the word 'mantra', the meaning of mantra, the classification of mantras, and the verbal definition or etymology of mantra.

Here I will just say that the meaning of the mantras of ultimate truth is that they protect the mind from names and concepts. The activities that go with this are the commitments associated with the body, speech, and mind of the buddhas. These are the activities of mantra. This is expounded in the *Later Secret Assembly Tantra*:

> Whatever mental attitude arises,
> Based on the senses and objects,
> Is explained as the meaning of *man*,
> While *tra* means the act of protecting.
> The commitments are that which is taught
> To free us from worldly activities.
> Being protected by all *vajras*
> Is explained as the meaning of mantra.

And:

> During the stages of empowerment
> The etymology of mantra is explained
> As the non-duality of emptiness and compassion.
> The way that emptiness and compassion
> Are non-dual and yet dual as well
> Is explained in what we call the secret mantra.

This is also expounded elsewhere, and can be studied in sources like the *Vajra Pinnacle*.

2.3. *Defining the* vajrayāna

This path is called *vajrayāna*. Here *vajra* means the *vajra* body, speech, and mind of the buddhas. And *yāna* refers to the path, because it is the means of travelling and the result, because it is the destination we travel towards. In that we travel the path by means of the *vajra* body, speech, and mind of the buddhas, this is a vehicle.

To begin with, while developing the awakening mind, one practises in a similar way to the path of the perfections. Then, when it is time to enter the *maṇḍala* and perform the empowerment, the master blesses the body, speech, and mind of the student as the *vajra* body, speech, and mind of the buddhas.

Next, while remaining inseparable from that experience, one meditates on the two stages of the path. At this time, one's experiences are transformed into the *vajra* body, speech, and mind of the buddhas. At that point one's own body, speech, and mind, and all of one's afflictions are the *vajra* essence. Understanding them as *vajra* becomes clearer and clearer through this practice. This is the path. When one attains the thirteenth stage, they manifest as the *vajra* body, speech, and mind. Because this is the destination one travels to, it is a *yāna*. This is also expounded in the *Secret Assembly Tantra*:

> Attachment, aversion, and ignorance
> Are permanently and joyfully established as *vajras*.
> Therefore this method of the buddhas
> Is called the *vajrayāna*.

2.4. *Defining it as the vehicle of the result*

When is this fully manifest *vajrayāna* achieved? A superior person will achieve it in this very lifetime, a middling person in the *bardo* (the intermediate state), an inferior person in seven rebirths, and a thoroughly inferior person in sixteen rebirths. The first type is mentioned in the *Secret Assembly Tantra*:

> With this method the great *dharma* person
> Emerges inseparable from the three buddha bodies.
> Ornamented with oceans of wisdom,
> Achievement will come in this very lifetime.

Achievement in the *bardo* has been expounded by my lama. It is also mentioned in the *Ornament of Realization*:

> Moreover, even those who have no diligence
> Will achieve it as soon as the body is abandoned.

In this passage, 'as soon as the body is abandoned' refers to the *bardo*. Achievement in seven rebirths is explained in the *Secret Treasury*:

> Those who have received empowerment and have true generosity
> Will receive empowerment in each subsequent rebirth.
> Because of this, in seven rebirths
> They will obtain accomplishments, even if they do not meditate.

Achievement in sixteen rebirths is explained in the *Five Commitments*:

> If there are no downfalls,
> It will be achieved in sixteen rebirths.

Are these achievements intended only for special people, or can ordinary people attain them as well? They can, as explained in the *Vajra Pinnacle*:

> According to the perfections,
> One does not attain the result for countless eons.
> But if yogins are diligent
> They can attain *nirvāṇa* in this very lifetime.
> Or, just by seeing the *maṇḍala*,
> They can attain *nirvāṇa* in sixteen rebirths.

So there is no question that ordinary people
Can attain buddhahood itself.

Thus this is called the vehicle of the result because the result can be achieved without difficulty. It is also called the vehicle of the result because one meditates on the aspect of the result right from the beginning. This is expounded in passages such as the following:

The five stages of manifest enlightenment
Are the virtuous personification of all buddhas.

For these reasons, in the secret mantra tradition, the path is fully realized along with the result at this very moment, and everything is completed at once. And it is called the vehicle of the result because it resembles the result, just as people call a very beautiful person a god. It is not the common path.

CHAPTER SEVEN

PRAYER

Liturgy of the Sixteen Elders

The practice of recitation in groups is a major part of Tibetan Buddhism, in both monastic and lay contexts. The liturgy translated here is a series of instructions for practice, written in the nineteenth century, which has at its centre a much earlier prayer, from the thirteenth century. The prayer The Ritual of the Sixteen Elders *was composed by the Kashmiri master Śākyaśrībhadra (1127–1225), who came to Tibet in the thirteenth century. This prayer is recited on occasions connected with Śākyamuni, particularly on the day on which his birth is celebrated annually.*

The practice of ritual is at the heart of Tibetan Buddhism. This begins with simple, day-to-day activities. Shrines in monasteries, temples, and people's homes are ornamented with offering bowls filled with rice or water that needs to be changed regularly. *Stūpas* representing the Buddha are circumambulated in a clockwise direction while thinking of the Buddha or one's lama and chanting mantras. Some texts suggest that where there are no *stūpas,* practitioners should imagine that the lama or Buddha is to their left, and that they are circumambulating as they walk, wherever they happen to be going.

For those who engage in regular meditation practice, there is the daily practice of *sādhana,* involving visualization and recitation of mantras, which are discussed in the previous chapter. There are also group practices, liturgies that are chanted on particular holy days. Liturgies are also chanted in groups at the request of those who wish to generate merit for themselves or others (a common instance being the illness or death of a relative). In the past, monks in the larger

Tibetan monasteries spent much of the day chanting these sorts of liturgies. These rituals are often referred to as *pūjā*. In fact, *pūjā* specifically means 'offerings', which is only one aspect, albeit an important one, of Buddhist liturgies. The proper name for the whole ritual is *vidhi* (in Tibetan, *cho ga*), and this is the genre of the text translated here, *A Brief Liturgy for the Ritual of the Sixteen Elders*.

Famed in Tibet as 'the Kashmiri Paṇḍita', Śākyaśrībhadra had already held high positions at the major Buddhist universities of India before coming to Tibet. In Tibet, he taught some of the major figures of various Buddhist schools, including Sakya Paṇḍita, who was to become the head of the Sakya school. The Kashmiri master also performed the full ordination ceremony for Sakya Paṇḍita, and his system of monastic vows (known as 'the Kashmiri system') became the most widespread in Tibet.

The sixteen elders (*sthavira*) of the title are a group of legendary figures associated with the historical Buddha Śākyamuni. They are all *arhats*, practitioners of the way of the hearers, who have attained an advanced spiritual state that is not yet that of a buddha. To this day the sixteen elders remain popular in Japan, whereas in China the group was expanded to eighteen. In Tibet and East Asia they are a popular subject of painting and sculpture.[1]

Aspects of ritual

Aspirational prayer

Aspirational prayers (*praṇidhāna*) are part of many Tibetan liturgies. In these prayers, which are usually in the first person, the practitioner states his or her own aspiration to attain the state of a buddha for the sake of all living beings. This is an expression of the vow of the bodhisattva, and its recitation is sometimes a practice in itself. More often, aspirational prayer provides the context and motivation for further recitation and visualization practices.

The most popular text in this genre is the *Aspirational Prayer of Samantabhadra*, which is drawn upon in the ritual described in this translation. One of the reasons for this prayer's popularity is that it invokes so many other ritual activities in its verses. The *Aspirational Prayer of Samantabhadra* brings together the 'seven branches' of prayer: paying homage; making offerings; repentance; confession; the request to the buddhas and bodhisattvas to teach; their request to remain in *saṃsāra*, and finally the dedication of merit.[2]

Homage and prostration

The physical act of prostration (bowing down until the body is flat on the ground) is an expression of the mental act of homage, and the Tibetan word *chagtsal* can be translated in both ways. Before bowing, the hands are placed together in the prayer position, and placed at the head, throat, and heart. This symbolizes that the act of homage is done with the full participation of one's body, speech, and mind. The act of prostration is performed when entering a shrine room, or the presence of a teacher. It is also performed as a practice in itself, while reciting a prayer for taking refuge, as part of the preliminary practices (*sngon 'gro*) of the *vajrayāna*. The main part of the text translated here, the prayer to the sixteen elders, is an extended act of paying homage.

Making offerings

The practice of making offerings is essentially a mental act that may or may not be accompanied by the presence of physical items to be offered. The ritual of making offerings (Skt. *pūjā,* Tib. *mchod pa*) is the central act of many group practices. In the text of the practice translated here, an idealized array of offerings is visualized, and the act of offering is accomplished by reciting a *dhāraṇī* (a Sanskrit incantation similar to a mantra). In *vajrayāna* initiations and preliminary practices, offerings are made in the form of the *maṇḍala* of the universe as known to Indian cosmology. This symbolic offering is usually made by placing precious stones or rice on a special metal plate representing the universe. The recipients of the offerings are the central figures of the practice, but as often as not, this is expanded to include all buddhas and bodhisattvas.

Repentance / confession

As discussed in chapters two and three, both lay and monastic Buddhists take vows. From the early days of Buddhism in India, monks and nuns gathered to confess any breakages of their vows in regular monthly or fortnightly ceremonies called *poṣadha,* during which the monastic regulations were also recited. Confession ceremonies are still central to the life of Tibetan monasteries. For lay practitioners, repentance and confession are incorporated into many practices, such as the liturgy translated here. In *vajrayāna* initiations and preliminary practices, the confession and purification of transgressions is accomplished through the visualization of the deity Vajrasattva.[3]

Rejoicing

Prayers of rejoicing are directed towards the great merit achieved by buddhas, bodhisattvas, and other religious practitioners, encouraging a sincere joy towards the good work of others. Such prayers are said to counter the negative emotion of jealousy.[4]

Entreating

The fifth and sixth aspects of the seven branches are entreaties directed towards buddhas, bodhisattvas, and teachers to teach, or 'turn the wheel of the *dharma*', and to remain in the world for as long as there are living beings to teach.

Dedication of merit

The dedication of the merit achieved through practice comes at the end of all Tibetan Buddhist liturgies; the dedication of the merit to all living beings identifying the practice as belonging to the greater vehicle as much as the bodhisattva's aspiration is stated at the beginning. Merit dedicated in this way is thought to contribute to the ultimate goal of bringing all living beings to enlightenment, rather than simply benefiting the person who does the practice. Individual acts of dedication are said to be like drops of water, gradually accumulating until they form an ocean; this metaphor appears in the dedication prayer of the liturgy translated here:

By bringing the oceans of merit to fullness,
Purifying the oceans of wisdom,
And filling the oceans of aspirational prayer,
May all beings become eminent noble ones.

How the practice works

The text translated here is a complete liturgy, compiled in the nineteenth century by one of the great figures of the era, Jamyang Khyentse Wangpo. His life and works are discussed in the next chapter. Khyentse Wangpo worked throughout his life to preserve and revitalize practices that were in danger of disappearing. A monk of the Sakya school, he also collected practices from other lineages, especially from the Nyingma and Kagyu schools. This version of the *Worship of the Sixteen Elders* is practised today in the Sakya school.

In this text, Khyentse Wangpo takes the famous prayer attributed to Śākyaśrībhadra, and constructs a liturgy around it based on other prayers. As there were so many texts already in circulation, this was a common way of creating a liturgy. Even when Khyentse Wangpo was composing liturgies himself, these usually incorporated some pre-existing prayers. A different version of this text, with the same main prayer but different beginnings and endings, is used in a ritual practised in the Gelug school.

Though Khyentse Wangpo's version of the liturgy is relatively short, it brings together all of the main ritual activities of Tibetan Buddhist liturgies. It begins with the prayers of taking refuge and generating the bodhisattva aspiration, the conventional opening of any *mahāyāna* Buddhist practice. Then the scene for the practice is set up with a visualization of a pure land, an idealized scene for the establishment of a relationship between the practitioners and the enlightened beings invoked by the practice. This is followed by the ritual invitation of the sixteen elders to 'come to this place'. This ritual of invitation, bringing the object of the ritual to the place where it is held, is found in Buddhist and non-Buddhist practices from India.

The actual prayer to the sixteen elders follows, after the verses of homage excerpted from the *Aspirational Prayer of Samantabhadra*. First Śākyamuni is invoked, then each of the sixteen elders, with their dwelling places, which form a map of the earthly and heavenly realms of Indian cosmology. Finally, the mythical kings who guard the four directions are invoked. This prayer extends the ritual act of homage and is followed by the other six aspects of the seven branches of prayer: making offerings, confession, rejoicing, the requests to teach and remain in *saṃsāra,* and the dedication of merit, all of these in further verses taken from the *Aspirational Prayer of Samantabhadra.*

The last part of the practice then moves from the realm of prayer to that of a *vajrayāna* meditation practice or *sādhana*. The practitioners visualize Śākyamuni surrounded by the sixteen elders and the four kings, and recite the mantra of Śākyamuni a hundred times or more. This act of visualization and recitation of a mantra is at the centre of *vajrayāna* practices. Here, it may be taken as an extension of the prayers already recited, or these prayers might be a prelude to the visualization and recitation practice. Thus Khyentse Wangpo's text allows a certain flexibility, depending on the context of its practice. The liturgy then ends in the conventional way with a dedication of merit and auspicious prayers.

As a final note on the practice, it is worth paying attention to the instructions that Khyentse Wangpo adds at various points. In the translation, these instructions are distinguished by being written in italics. He instructs the practitioner, while reciting the prayer and *dhāraṇī* for making offerings at the beginning of the practice, to 'Recite the *Clouds of Offerings dhāraṇī* three times, while playing musical instruments and burning and circulating incense'. The presence of music – usually cymbals and drums, and sometimes horns – and incense engages the senses more fully in the practice.

A BRIEF LITURGY FOR THE WORSHIP OF THE SIXTEEN ELDERS

Om Swasti. This is a brief liturgy for the ritual connected with the worship of the elders, which is said to have been composed by the great Paṇḍita Śākyaśrī.

Refuge and the awakening mind

Recite the following three times:

To the supreme ones, the Buddha, *dharma* and *sangha,*
I go for refuge until enlightenment.
By the merit of my practice of generosity and the rest,
May I achieve buddhahood for the sake of beings.

The fourfold aspiration

May all sentient beings have happiness and the causes of happiness.
May they be separate from suffering and the causes of suffering.
May they never be separate from the sublime happiness free from suffering.
May they abide in the great equanimity that is free from attachment and aversion.

Visualizing the pure realm

By the power of the genuine places of refuge, the three jewels,
The blessings of the buddhas and bodhisattvas,
And the space of reality possessing the two accumulations,

A vast and beautiful jeweled palace
Is established in a land of bliss,
Containing a precious lion throne with lotus and moon seats,
And filled like an ocean with arrays of offerings,
Both real and emanated by the power of the *dhāraṇī.*

Recite the Clouds of Offerings dhāraṇī *three times, while playing musical instruments and burning and circulating incense*:

Namo ratnatrayaya
Om namo bhagawate benza sara pramadhani tatagataya
Arhate samyaksam buddhaya tadyata
Om benze benze maha benze mahatezo benze
Mahabodichitta benze mahabodisatto benze
Mahabodhimando pasam tramana benze
Sarvakarma awarana bishodhana benze
Soha[5]

Invitation

In the centre of a plain, as flat as the hand's palm,
Bedecked with jewels and adorned with trees and lakes,
Is a jeweled palace with four corners and four doors.
Upon a throne with lotus, sun, and moon seats,
Is seated the protector of beings who with compassion
Places students in these troubled times on the way to liberation.
Supreme sage, great elders, and your retinue,
Please come to this place.

All buddhas and bodhisattvas of the ten directions,
Whose blazing fire of insight dries up the ocean of negative emotions,
Fields of liberation and merit, we attend upon you.
Assembly of monks from the ten directions, please remain here.

Accepting this invitation to this place of offerings,
Please come and take these offerings for the sake of living beings.

The protector of beings, the lion of the Śākyas
Has placed the Buddha's teaching in your hands,
And you have opened the treasure chest of scripture –
Great *arhats* who maintain the *dharma*, please remain here.
By this invitation for you to propagate the *dharma*,
Please come and take these offerings for the sake of living beings.

Entrusted by the sage with the victory banner of the teachings:
Aṅgaja, Ajita and Vanavāsin,
Kālika, Vajrīputra and Śrībhadra,
Kanakavatsa and Kanakabharadvaja,
Noble Bakula and Rāhula,
Kṣudrapanthaka and Piṇḍolabharadvaja,
Panthaka, Nāgasena, Gopaka, and Abhedya:
Oh great *arhat* elders,
By this invitation, oh precious islands of merit,
Please come and take these offerings for the sake of living beings.[6]

Though you are buddhas with perfect renunciation and wisdom,
You adopt the style of hearers for the sake of trainees.
You whose special activity is to maintain the *dharma*,
Sixteen elders, please remain in this place.

Protecting and raising high the transmitted words of the *tathāgatas*,
In the forest of *saṃsāra* you have abandoned all self-interest,
You devote yourselves to the benefit of others, oh sixteen elders,
By the power of your vow of compassion, please come to this place.

Lay practitioners who requested refuge with honest words of truth,
You asked to act as servants to the three jewels.
By this invitation, oh fields of precious merit,
Please come and take these offerings for the sake of living beings.

Perform the invitation with music.

Homage

Throughout all the worlds in the ten directions
And the three times, oh *tathāgatas*, lions among men,
To all of you, without a single exception,
I sincerely pay homage with my body, speech, and mind.

By the power of the aspirational prayer of excellent conduct,
Holding all of the conquerors clearly in mind,
And bowing with as many bodies as there are atoms in the world,
I completely pay homage to all the conquerors.

With as many buddhas on a single atom as there are atoms in the world,
Each one seated in the middle of a circle of bodhisattvas,
I visualize the whole space of reality
Filled with all of the conquerors.

With inexhaustible oceans of praise,
And in every melody from the ocean of harmonies,
I recite the qualities of all the conquerors
Eulogizing all those who have gone to bliss.[7]

Prayer to the sixteen elders

I pay homage to the incomparable one whom we never tire of looking upon,

Your body resplendent in colours of gold,
With one face and two arms, sitting with crossed legs,
One hand touching the ground, the other in the meditation position.
So that the life of the lama may be stable,
And the teachings spread, please grant your blessings.

Homage to the noble elder Aṅgaja,
Dwelling on the vast snowy mountain of Kailash,
Surrounded by one thousand three hundred *arhats*,
Holding an incense burner and fly whisk.
So that the life of the lama may be stable,
And the teachings spread, please grant your blessings.

Homage to the noble elder Ajita,
Dwelling on Black Crystal Mountain, home of the sages,
Surrounded by a hundred *arhats*,
His two hands in the meditation position.
So that the life of the lama may be stable,
And the teachings spread, please grant your blessings.

Homage to the noble elder Vanavāsin,
Dwelling in a cave on the Seven Leaf Mountain,
Surrounded by one thousand four hundred *arhats*,
Holding a fly whisk and making the gesture of threat.
So that the life of the lama may be stable,
And the teachings spread, please grant your blessings.

Homage to the noble elder Kālika,
Dwelling in the land of copper in the Rose Apple continent,
Surrounded by one thousand one hundred *arhats*,
Holding golden earrings.
So that the life of the lama may be stable,
And the teachings spread, please grant your blessings.

Homage to the noble elder Vajrīputra,
Dwelling in the land of Śrī Laṅka,
Surrounded by a thousand great *arhats,*
Holding a fly whisk and making the gesture of threat.
So that the life of the lama may be stable,
And the teachings spread, please grant your blessings.

Homage to the noble elder Śrībhadra,
Dwelling in the land of the Yamunā River Valley,
Surrounded by one thousand two hundred *arhats,*
One hand in the teaching gesture, the other in the meditation position.
So that the life of the lama may be stable,
And the teachings spread, please grant your blessings.

Homage to the noble elder Kanakavatsa,
Dwelling in holy land of Kashmir,
Surrounded by five hundred great *arhats,*
Holding a string of jewels.
So that the life of the lama may be stable,
And the teachings spread, please grant your blessings.

Homage to the noble elder Kanakabharadvaja,
Dwelling in the Bountiful Cow continent,
Surrounded by seven hundred great *arhats,*
With both hands in the meditation position.
So that the life of the lama may be stable,
And the teachings spread, please grant your blessings.

Homage to the noble elder Bakula,
Dwelling in the Discordant Sound continent,
Surrounded by nine hundred great *arhats,*
Holding a mongoose with both hands.
So that the life of the lama may be stable,
And the teachings spread, please grant your blessings.

Homage to the noble elder Rāhula,
Dwelling in the land of Priyaṅgu,
Surrounded by one thousand one hundred *arhats,*
Holding a jeweled crown.
So that the life of the lama may be stable,
And the teachings spread, please grant your blessings.

Homage to the noble elder Kṣudrapanthaka,
Dwelling on the Vulture Peak Mountain,
Surrounded by one thousand six hundred *arhats,*
With both hands in the meditation position.
So that the life of the lama may be stable,
And the teachings spread, please grant your blessings.

Homage to the noble elder Piṇḍolabharadvaja,
Dwelling in the Noble Form continent,
Surrounded by a thousand *arhats,*
Holding a book and a begging bowl.
So that the life of the lama may be stable,
And the teachings spread, please grant your blessings.

Homage to the noble elder Panthaka,
Dwelling in the Heaven of Thirty-Three,
Surrounded by nine hundred noble *arhats,*
Making the gesture of teaching and holding a book.
So that the life of the lama may be stable,
And the teachings spread, please grant your blessings.

Homage to the noble elder Nāgasena,
Dwelling on the slopes of Mount Meru,
Surrounded by one thousand two hundred *arhats,*
Holding a vase and monk's staff.
So that the life of the lama may be stable,
And the teachings spread, please grant your blessings.

Homage to the noble elder Gopaka,
Dwelling on the king of mountains Bihula,
Surrounded by one thousand four hundred *arhats,*
Holding a book with both hands.
So that the life of the lama may be stable,
And the teachings spread, please grant your blessings.

Homage to the noble elder Abhedya,
Dwelling on the king of mountains, Himālaya,
Surrounded by a thousand *arhats,*
Holding a *stūpa* of enlightenment.
So that the life of the lama may be stable,
And the teachings spread, please grant your blessings.

Homage to the noble layman Dharmatāra,
His hair in a topknot, books on his back,
Visualizing Amitābha in the sky before him,
He holds a fly whisk and a vase.
So that the life of the lama may be stable,
And the teachings spread, please grant your blessings.[8]

Homage to the four great kings,
Empowered by donning the armour of effort,
Guarding the excellent teachings of the Buddha,
In the east, the south, the west, and the north.
So that the life of the lama may be stable,
And the teachings spread, please grant your blessings.

Recite this three times or as much as you are able.

Offerings

The best garlands of the best flowers,
Symbols, perfumed ointments, and finest parasols,

The finest lamps, and the best incense:
These I offer to the conquerors.

The best garments and the finest perfumes,
Jars of medicinal powders as high as Mount Meru,
All beautifully and perfectly arranged:
These I offer to the conquerors.

These vast and unsurpassable offerings,
I visualize alongside all of the conquerors,
And by the power of confidence in excellent conduct,
I perform prostrations and offerings to all of the conquerors.[9]

Namo ratnatrayaya
Om namo bhagawate benza sara pramadhani tatagataya
Arhate samyaksam buddhaya tadyata
Om benze benze maha benze mahatezo benze
Mahabodichitta benze mahabodisatto benze
Mahabodhimando pasam tramana benze
Sarvakarma awarana bishodhana benze
Soha

Recite this along with music. Optionally, it is acceptable to make a maṇḍala *offering.*

Confession

Under the sway of attachment, aversion, and ignorance,
Whatever negative actions I have performed,
With my body, speech, and mind,
I confess them all, one by one.

Rejoicing

All the conquerors and bodhisattvas,
Solitary buddhas, trainees, and those beyond training,

And all living beings:
I sincerely rejoice in their merit.

Request to teach

Those who light up the worlds of the ten directions,
Who have attained buddhahood through gradual
enlightenment,
I request these protectors, for the sake of all beings,
To turn the incomparable wheel of *dharma*.

Prayer to remain

Those who have shown the way to *nirvāṇa*,
For the welfare and happiness of all beings,
With hands together I pray for them to stay
For as many eons as there are atoms in the world.

Dedication

Whatever small merit I have accumulated
Through prostration, offering, and confession,
Rejoicing, requesting, and praying,
I dedicate to enlightenment for all.

Recite the dhāraṇī*:*

Namo ratnatrayaya
Om namo bhagawate benza sara pramadhani tatagataya
Arhate samyaksam buddhaya tadyata
Om benze benze maha benze mahatezo benze
Mahabodichitta benze mahabodisatto benze
Mahabodhimando pasam tramana benze
Sarvakarma awarana bishodhana benze
Soha

Invocation

Calling on the names of Śākyamuni and his entourage, I invoke their commitments.

Visualize them, and with one-pointed devotion, recite:

Om muni muni mahamuni shakyamuniye soha

Recite this a hundred times or as much as you are able.

Assembly of great *arhats*, emanations of the buddhas,
Who guard the teachings for the sake of beings,
Sixteen elders, who embody the three jewels,
Grant your blessings that the *dharma* might long endure.

Sixteen elders, whose nature is compassion,
Who have crossed the ocean of *saṃsāra* and ended negative emotions,
With the assembly of sixteen thousand four hundred *arhats*,
Grant your blessings that the *dharma* might long endure.

Arhats who bring good fortune to sentient beings,
Eminent and gracious, worthy of every being's gifts,
Oh you great persons, noble ones,
Grant your blessings that the *dharma* might long endure.

Dedication of merit

May the basis of virtuous behaviour in myself and others
Spread the teachings, the source of happiness and well being,
And abolishing all the sources of suffering,
Swiftly dry up the oceans of existence.

By bringing the oceans of merit to fullness,
Purifying the oceans of wisdom,
And filling the oceans of aspirational prayer,
May all beings become eminent noble ones.

Prayer for auspiciousness

He has completed the two accumulations and accomplished the activities
Of the buddhas of the three times, being indistinguishable from them,
And he brings his students, equal in their good fortune, to ripeness:
May the auspiciousness of the supreme lama without equal be present here.

With the compassion of the buddhas of the three times and the bodhisattvas,
Adopting the style of hearers until existence exists no longer,
Protecting the teachings and working for the benefit of beings:
May the auspiciousness of the great elders be present here.

They whose gaze goes deep and far,
Dhṛtarāṣṭra, Virūḍhaka,
Virūpākṣa, and Vaiśravaṇa:
May the auspiciousness of the four great kings be present here.

Sole source of happiness and well-being,
May the teachings long endure,
And may the great beings who uphold the teachings,
Hold firm the victory banner of their lives.

By the coming of the Teacher into this world,
By his teachings as bright as the sun,
And by the harmony of the disciples who uphold his teachings,

May the auspiciousness of the long-abiding teachings be present here.

Recite auspicious prayers such as this, and finish with music.

This was written by Mañjughoṣa. May all be auspicious.

CHAPTER EIGHT

THE LIFE OF A MASTER

Jamyang Khyentse Wangpo

Reading the life stories of great Buddhist practitioners of the past is an important practice in Tibetan Buddhism. These stories offer inspiration, as well as models of how to behave as a monk or lay practitioner. Here, the verse autobiography of the nineteenth-century master Jamyang Khyentse Wangpo (1820–92) is translated. Though brief, it offers a detailed account of the external activities, internal development, and the secret dreams and visions of one of the most revered teachers in the Tibetan Buddhist tradition. He devoted his life to collecting and printing rare texts for practices that were in danger of dying out, ultimately preserving them from destruction in the following century. His approach to collecting and publishing these texts was not limited by sectarian affiliation; he was recognized as a reborn lama in the Sakya school, took his monastic vows in a Nyingma monastery, and collected teachings from the other main schools as well. This approach influenced other teachers and scholars, and came to be known as the rimé *or 'non-partisan' approach.*

Biography in Tibetan Buddhism

The ideals of Tibetan Buddhism are embodied ideals. The removal of personal obstructions to one's innate wisdom, and the way this wisdom manifests as compassionate activity is illustrated in the lives of great practitioners. Thus the way that the Buddha's teachings can be realized through practice is taught in Tibetan Buddhism through the biographies of previous masters. Some biographies have been particularly important in Tibet's culture. The life and songs of the hermit Milarepa are especially revered as both an illustration of the path to realization and a series of teachings that can help anyone to reach that goal. Milarepa's story tells of his bad beginnings in black magic and murder, his great regret and striving to make up for his crimes, his unswerving devotion to his teacher Marpa, his renunciation of worldly things for the life of a solitary hermit, and his wisdom expressed in song.

Milarepa's life and songs, written in the fifteenth century, are classics of religious literature, but are not really representative of Tibetan biographies in general, which tend to have less of a compelling narrative. Nevertheless, biographies of particular masters are sources of both information and inspiration for practitioners in a lineage that leads back to that master. In this way, biographies remain closely linked with practice, and the reading of biographies is another form of religious practice.

Biographies of Tibetan masters work on several levels, which are sometimes separated out into three aspects of a life. First is the outer biography, which records the activities of the subject and includes the usual major biographical events such as birth, education, career, and death. For a Buddhist teacher, the outer biography is mainly concerned with their career, which should encompass the three spheres of activity: renunciation, study, and good works. Second, the inner biography concerns the internal life of the subject, specifically, their meditation practice and its effect on their spiritual development. Third, the secret biography is a record of visions and dreams that are considered relevant to the subject's spiritual development. These visions may also include intimations of previous lives, tying the subject of the biography into the Tibetan Buddhist tradition.

The text translated here is a brief autobiography by the nineteenth-century master Jamyang Khyentse Wangpo. The Tibetan name of this text, *Directly Spoken*, indicates that it was written by, or at least based on an interview with, its subject. Though many Tibetan teachers have written extensive autobiographies, Jamyang Khyentse Wangpo did not. This brief account in verse is all we have, though much longer biographies were subsequently written by others.[1]

The life of Jamyang Khyentse Wangpo

Jamyang Khyentse Wangpo was born into two wealthy and influential Derge families. In *Directly Spoken* he mentions miracles that were said to accompany his birth; later biographies list these in detail, including all the water in the house turning into milk, and rainbow-hued clouds appearing in the sky. He also mentions his own early visions of protector deities, such as the six-armed Mahākāla, guarding him.

Khyentse Wangpo's father was an official at the Derge court, and he had his son educated in preparation for government service. His mother taught him to write, and his father taught him the calligraphic skills needed by government officials. He also learned astrology and medicine, and studied Sanskrit grammar and poetics. But a career in the Derge civil service was not to be. When Khyentse was twelve, an abbot from the Sakya monastery of Ngor in central Tibet paid a visit to the family home, and recognized the boy as the rebirth of a previous abbot.

This suggests that the abbot thought Khyentse Wangpo too good to be lost to a career in government service. Only by recognizing him as a reborn lama, or *tulku,* could the monastery be sure that he would not be claimed by the king. At the age of twenty Khyentse fulfilled his duties by travelling to Ngor monastery and receiving teachings from the head abbot. But rather than staying at Ngor, he travelled to the Nyingma monastery of Mindroling to receive his monastic vows there instead.

Having received his vows, Khyentse Wangpo began his great project, which would occupy the next thirteen years. He set off with a few provisions and one monk attendant, visiting monasteries and sacred sites across Tibet. His aim was now to collect as many Buddhist texts as he could, but this was not just a matter of collecting physical books. As we have seen in previous chapters, religious texts are rarely studied or put into practice in Tibetan Buddhism without a ritual transmission, which must be given by somebody who has themselves previously received the transmission.

Thus when Khyentse Wangpo says in *Directly Spoken* that he received the transmissions for over seven hundred volumes, this doesn't mean only the finding and collecting of the books, but also sitting and listening to seven hundred volumes being read aloud. And this was not done in one place, but in monasteries, hermitages, and caves all over Tibet. In this way Khyentse collected hundreds of rare transmissions that would otherwise have died out within a generation or two.

These transmissions were mainly from lineages that had been sidelined by the Gelug school, which had grown in power over the previous two centuries and now dominated central Tibet. The Sakya school was far from the force it had once been in Tibet, and some of the minor Kagyu lineages were close to extinction. With characteristic humility, Khyentse Wangpo says: 'I put only a handful of these into practice, and understood just the basics.'

When Khyentse finally returned to Derge for good he was thirty-three years old. He set up his own temple with a small but comfortable room in which to live, meditate, and teach, and swore never to cross the threshold again. Most of the rest of Khyentse's life was spent in these small meditation quarters. Together with the other most important figure in the cultural revival of eastern Tibet, Jamgon Kongtrul Lodro Taye (1813–99), he worked to edit and publish the rare texts he had gathered. The great printing house at Derge printed volume after volume of the *Compendium of Tantras* and the *Treasury of Precious Terma*. Khyentse singles out Jamgon Kongtrul for praise in his autobiography.[2]

In his autobiography, Khyentse Wangpo mentions this work as one among many of his activities, which also included commissioning statues for monasteries and funding the construction of *stūpas*. The wealth that Khyentse Wangpo used for these religious works mostly came from donations from his patrons. After a major war broke out in Derge, he used these funds to help rebuild the monasteries. He also made regular donations of tea bricks to monasteries, which was a way of funding the practice of rituals, as butter tea was served to monks in the main hall of the monastery. By describing these offerings in his autobiography, Khyentse shows that he fulfilled all three of the activities expected of a teacher: renunciation, study, and good works.[3]

Meditation and visions

The three spheres of activity expected of a teacher form Khyentse's outer biography. The inner biography is a record of meditation practice and the spiritual transformation that it brings. In this Khyentse describes how he put his non-partisan approach into practice in his own meditation, gathering and practising the meditation traditions known as the 'eight great chariots'. He merely touches on the fact that he meditated on these traditions, and experienced visions and other signs of accomplishment. He explains his reluctance to say more as a concern not to boast and seem attached to his own accomplishments: 'to speak extensively would diminish the importance of non-attachment.'

The secret autobiography records some of the key visions of Khyentse Wangpo's spiritual career. Two great visions are spoken of in some detail. The first, in his fifteenth year, was of the Indian master Mañjuśrīmitra, who is associated with the bodhisattva Mañjuśrī, embodiment of intelligence and wisdom, and is also one of the key figures in the *dzogchen* tradition. These two aspects of Mañjuśrīmitra are symbolized in the vision by the two books that he holds in his hands. Khyentse Wangpo's second vision, which he had in the following year, was of Padmasambhava, the tantric master who visited Tibet in the eighth century and became, for the Nyingma school, an embodiment of enlightenment.

These two visions emphasize Khyentse Wangpo's commitment to the view and practice of *dzogchen*, 'the great perfection'. *Dzogchen* is a complex of contemplative practices and poetic writings in Tibetan Buddhism. The three series of *dzogchen* mentioned by Khyentse Wangpo are the mind series, the space series, and the esoteric instruction series. Though each series has its own approach, they all emphasize the immediate presence of the enlightened state of mind and the need to give up effort and striving in the attempt to achieve enlightenment. A verse spoken by Padmasambhava in the vision related here summarizes the practice:

> Untainted by grasped objects,
> Uncorrupted by grasping thoughts,
> Maintaining naked awareness and emptiness:
> That's the enlightened mind of all buddhas.

Appended to the outer, inner, and secret autobiographies is a personal account of Khyentse Wangpo's previous lives. Another aspect of Khyentse Wangpo's activities was the revelation of hidden treasures or *terma* (*gter ma*), which are teachings considered to have been concealed in the past for the benefit of future generations. Several kinds of hidden treasure are mentioned here, including those buried in the ground or inside rocks (earth treasures) and those concealed in the continuum of the mind (mind treasures). Most treasures are said to have been concealed by Padmasambhava during the reign of the emperor Tri Song Detsen in the ninth century.[4]

The previous lives mentioned by Khyentse Wangpo here connect him with the *terma* tradition, including two figures from Tibet's imperial period, the emperor Tri Song Detsen and the prince Chogdrup Gyalpo, and famous treasure revealers. Finally, Khyentse Wangpo speaks of his own death as a union with another figure from Tibet's imperial period, the adept Vimalamitra. He prophesies that five emanations will emerge to carry on his work, and this will take place at 'the five-peaked mountain', which is Wutaishan in China, famous throughout Asia as the dwelling place of the bodhisattva Mañjuśrī. A number of influential teachers were recognized as emanations of Khyentse Wangpo after his death, including Dzongsar Khyentse Chokyi Lodro (1893–1959) and Dilgo Khyentse Tashi Paljor (1910–91).[5]

Today, Jamyang Khyentse Wangpo's legacy is seen in the great collections of texts that came from his work and inspiration of others, and the idea of a non-partisan Buddhism. Teachings that he authored or collected are practised in all the schools of Tibetan Buddhism, and his life story, like that of Milarepa, is held up as an example of what can be accomplished with devotion to the Buddhist teachings. The text of this brief autobiography is located in the massive twenty-four volume series of Jamyang Khyentse Wangpo's collected works. It occurs at the end of a cycle of texts called *Rain of Wisdom: The Guru Yoga of the Three Buddha Bodies*. This liturgical cycle includes several guru yoga texts – devotional practices focussed on teachers from the past, from recent figures to Padmasambhava and Tri Song Detsen from Tibet's imperial period. This shows how even the genre of biography is completely integrated into religious practice.

THE ESSENTIAL BIOGRAPHY OF JAMYANG KHYENTSE WANGPO

Out of reverence for my glorious lama,
The lord of the ocean-like three jewels and roots,
I will give a brief and accurate summary
Without exaggerating or denigrating my own character.

The outer biography

I was born in Eastern Derge, in Greater Tibet,
In the area known as Terlhung,
At the foot of the cliff called Great Garuda,
Into two well-known families
In the fourteenth iron dragon year,
In the six month of summer,
On the day on which the wheel of the *dharma* was turned,
The day that completes the waxing moon,
Accompanied by miraculous signs, so they say.

My earliest memories are of wisdom guardians,
The six-armed one, and Ekajaṭī,
Watching over and protecting me again and again.
I had vague memories of the imprints of my previous lives,
And from when I was little I would hang around renunciates.[6]

In my twenty-first year I travelled to U,
And in the great island of teachings that ripen and liberate,
My spiritual guide, the perfectly steadfast and learned

Rigzin Zangpo, gave me the full ordination.
Then the throne-holder Sangye Kunga bestowed upon me
The bodhisattva vow of the *madhyamaka* tradition,
And the empowerments of Śrī Viśuddha in the So tradition,
And the *Heart Essence of the Vidyādharas.*
Thus I became a holder of the three kinds of vow.[7]

Then in the three realms of Kham, U and Tsang,
For thirteen years I searched for teachings,
Studying with a hundred and fifty crown jewels,
Including *vajrayāna* practitioners and spiritual guides,
And experts in the sciences.
Along with craftsmanship and healing, and all the branches of grammar and logic,
I studied the traditions of commentary on the *vinaya, abhidharma, madhyamaka* and *prajñāpāramitā.*

I received over seven hundred volumes in total:
The scriptures and treasures containing
The empowerments, blessings, and permissions
Of the new and old *vajrayāna* lineages,
The oral instructions for ripening and liberating
Found among the uncorrupted traditions of Kadam and Sakyapa,
Drikung, Taklung, Tsurpu, and Drugpa.
As a support, commentaries on tantras such as
Hevajra and *Cakrasaṃvara,* the *Secret Assembly,*
The *Wheel of Time,* the *Magical Net,* and the *Secret Matrix,*
And the transmissions for the scriptures of the Kanjur and Tenjur.[8]

In brief, I received the lineages of the long traditions
Of the ten chariots of tantric exposition,
Practising merely a handful of them and understanding just the basics.
This great stream of *dharma* that I received,

The doctrines of my own school and others too,
I mostly taught as well, again and again,
Though never in the hope of remuneration.

From the highest of holy saints
To the humblest of ordinary folk,
I spread gifts of *dharma* day and night, as much as I could.
I did this from a heartfelt aspiration and intention
To encourage the flow of the teachings.

To represent the Buddha's body,
I commissioned two thousand statues
All made from gilded copper.

To represent the Buddha's speech,
I had forty volumes printed,
And if you combine manuscripts with printed books
I commissioned about two thousand books in all.
Beautifully published copies of these books
Were placed in thirteen temples.

As representations of the Buddha's mind,
I commissioned over a hundred *stūpas*
Made of gilded copper,
Including one great *stūpa*,
And I donated *stūpas* whenever I could.[9]

When I established a new permanent residence,
It was difficult to finish it in time,
And I could not put enough effort into printing.
At this point, war broke out in Lower Do,
And most of the monasteries were damaged.
At the request of religious leaders of China and Tibet,

And the lords and ministers of Derge,
I was appointed to raise funds to repair them.

For my own part, making offerings from head to toe,
I donated over three thousand bricks of tea.
Much was accomplished through dedicated activity,
And most of the monasteries were rebuilt or repaired.[10]

The *dharma* communities of the area
Came together every year
To recite *dhāraṇīs*, mantras, prayers, and dedications;
At these times I donated bricks of tea,
Over four thousand in total,
For the benefit of everyone who took part.

To a vast gathering
Of spiritual guides beyond number
Including great sages and holders of the teachings,
From the Sakya, Kagyu, Nyingma, and Gelug schools,
Headed by the chief minister of the Sino-Tibetan lands,
I gave the offering of *dharma*,
Empowerments and blessings to remove obstacles,
Fulfilling the wishes of those whose minds were weary.
In every place I visited
I dispersed clouds of offerings.

Along with having faith and devotion
Towards every one of our philosophical systems,
I have very few misconceptions,
And so I have been able to have
Extensive contact with Bon teachers.
And though it was difficult for them to change
And enter fully into meditation,
By practising a little, these students

Did not think of performing village rituals,
And the like, even in their dreams.
Giving up thoughts of this life,
They came to understand the way of the mendicant.[11]

I met with people whether they were high or lowly,
And helped to resolve their tangled hopes and fears.
Throughout my life, from the age of thirteen,
I performed the yogic meditation of my personal deity,
And meditated on hundreds of profound instructions.
Thanks to this, visions and realizations came to me.

If I ever spent time not in solitude,
It was only to fulfill a promise or expectation.
I have been through both bad times and good,
But my mind has always been at peace.
This was a brief summary of my outer biography,
Of the three spheres of a teacher's activity.[12]

The inner biography

My mind was full of the greatest faith and devotion
Towards the eight great chariots of the practice lineage:
The Early Translations, the Kadam, the Sakyapa,
The Marpa and Shangpa Kagyu, the Six Practices,
Pacification, Cutting, and Deity Yoga.

Many of these traditions had declined in recent times,
So, striving against great difficulties time and time again,
I found many of them and received the transmissions.[13]
Studying, contemplating and meditating upon them,
In reality, in visions, and in dreams,
I received instruction through the direct transmissions
Of lamas, deities, and *ḍākiṇis*,
And came to see everything as a blessing.

It is indeed hard to achieve true accomplishment,
But I understood and mastered
The meanings of the texts and the methods of meditation.
Since it is difficult to delve into another's mind,
I have kept this brief; to speak extensively
Would diminish the importance of non-attachment.
So, for now I speak these words
As mere seeds of an inner biography.

The secret biography

As it has been said again and again
In the prophecies of the Great Orgyen,
In the eighth year of my life
I suffered from a severe illness.
At that time Pema Totreng and his consort
Appeared, and freed me from my troubles
With the blessing and empowerment of Vajrakīlaya.[14]

In my fifteenth year I had a vision so clear and stable
It was hard to tell whether it was real or illusory.
I found myself in Vajrāsana
In front of a nine-storeyed pagoda.
I climbed the stairs to the eighth floor,
Where I met the master Mañjuśrīmitra,
Who looked like an Indian *Paṇḍita,*
With a book on his left and another on his right.[15]

When I bowed with devotion and made a request,
He immediately picked up the book on his left,
Which seemed to be a Sanskrit manuscript
Of the *Summation of the Perfection of Wisdom,*
And placed it on the top of my head, saying,
'This is the full blessing
Of the transmission of the dialectical *dharma.*'

The book on his right was a *dzogchen* work,
Called *The Heart Mirror of Vajrasattva.*
With it he conferred the full blessing and significance
Of the general methods of mantra blessings
And the three series of *dzogchen.*[16]

Finally, he gave some prophecies
And was joyfully absorbed into light,
Which dissolved into me,
And for a time I remained in a non-conceptual state.
Then as turned to leave, I found a great fire in the
doorway;
Powerlessly I entered the blaze
And my gross body was immediately incinerated.
I appeared in a brilliant body made of light
With the thought 'I am Vimalamitra!'

At other times I met with many great adepts,
Such as Tangtong Gyalpo,
And received empowerments and blessings,
Great accomplishments embodying the Heart Essence.[17]

In my sixteenth year, on the tenth day of the Saga month,
I found myself one morning in the Palace of Lotus Light.
Suddenly I was atop a sparkling mountain peak,
Surrounded by extremely beautiful white clouds,
Where I met the Lake Born One with an entourage of *ḍākiṇis.*
With his enlightened mind he granted blessings and symbolic
empowerments,
And conferred a prophecy about the seven transmissions.

Finally, adopting a yogic gaze, he proclaimed:
'Untainted by grasped objects,
Uncorrupted by grasping thoughts,

Maintaining naked awareness and emptiness:
That's the enlightened mind of all buddhas.'

With that, he dissolved into me,
His mind merging inseparably with mine,
And I stood in my own place in the state of reality.
Since then, whenever I have had conceptual elaborations
I have prayed with one-pointed devotion,
And thanks to this, have received the transmissions
Of the whole scriptural tradition of the early translations,
Earth treasures and rediscovered treasures,
Mind treasures, pure visions and aural transmissions,
And treasures of recollection.[18]

Praise for Jamgon Kongtrul

Jamgon Kongtrul Lodro Taye
Is the great translator Vairocana in person,
The benevolent embodiment of a hundred buddhas,
The greatest chariot of *dharma* in the Jambu continent.
Although he has already understood most things,
He spreads wonderful clouds of offerings and joy.

I asked him to stay with me and help publish
The *Treasury of Precious Terma*,
Along with its supplement, the *Wondrous Sayings*.
Because he has practised and taught yogic meditation,
All of his actions are meaningful.
Furthermore, he gives offerings and joy
To whoever is in need, without partiality.[19]

Conclusion

The beginnings of all of this
Are to be seen in prophetic utterances and inventories.

The middle has now been written down,
And the end will depend on how things come about
And my own practice.

If I was to explain in great detail
The methods of the empowerments and blessings of
My masters, personal deities, and the *ḍākiṇis*,
I would never be able to elaborate upon
What one should know, not even to explain a fraction
Of all the different classes of the *dharma*.
In the future, there may be the opportunity for further
elaboration,
But for now I offer this biography,
Brief as it is,
As mere seeds of the essential points.

Previous lives

I have little power to remember my previous lives,
But in order to clarify the treasure transmissions
And because greater people than I might take pleasure in it,
I will pass this on.

The prayers invoking their previous lives
Written by glorious beings like the Karmapa are clear and distinct;
These are just my random impressions.

I am clear about certain *paṇḍitas* and *siddhas*:
Vajraghaṇṭapa,
Anantamukhamati,
And the great *paṇḍita* Vanaratna.[20]

In Tibet, though I have only a few scattered recollections,
I am fairly certain of some, including

Tri Song Detsen and Chogdrup Gyalpo,
Guru Chowang and Ngari Paṇḍita,
Tangtong Gyalpo and the great Lhatsun.[21]

In the future, while practising the guru yoga of Vimalamitra,
I will pass from this life, and as soon as I do,
I will dissolve into the heart of the great *Paṇḍita* Vimalamitra.
Then at the five-peaked mountain, the place of emanation,
By the power of my aspirations five emanations will emerge,
To benefit the teaching in a non-partisan way (*rimé*), thus it has been spoken.

Dedication

This account of my lives throughout the three times
I offer to Khetsun Zangpo,
Who is the emanation of Jigme Trinley Ozer,
The final birth of Prince Damzin,
A universal emperor of unsurpassed accomplishments.

Jigme Tenpai Nyima, with the gift of a silk ceremonial scarf,
Asked me earnestly, and because I could not turn my back on him,
This was written by me, Jamyang Khyentse Wangpo,
As the very briefest of summaries, a mere seed.

By the virtue of this, till we attain the essence of enlightenment,
May we never be separate from the supreme vehicle and spiritual guides,
And may we swiftly attain enlightenment.[22]

Colophon

If you pray fervently from the heart
To Lama Jamyang Khyentse Wangpo,

Holding him close until you attain enlightenment,
Then you will be blessed so your mind merges with his.

This was said by the worthy and devoted rebirth of our sublime accomplished leader, Tsewang Lhamo, concerning the virtue and auspiciousness of Jamyang Khyentse Wangpo's writings.

NOTES

CHAPTER 1. AN INTRODUCTION TO THE PRACTICE OF TIBETAN BUDDHISM

1. Here, I use 'Tibet' to refer to the parts of modern China where the inhabitants have historically considered themselves Tibetans and which share a culture bound by Tibetan language and customs. I have discussed this in van Schaik 2011: xvii–xviii. On Buddhism in Mongolia, see Wallace 2015.
2. This list of four schools is somewhat misleading, as the Nyingma ('old ones') refers to a whole complex of practice lineages going back to the time of the Tibetan empire, and the Kagyu is divided into many sub-schools. The Sakya and Gelug may be more accurately called schools, but here too there are internal distinctions, characterized by affiliations to particular monastic lineages.
3. While the bodhisattva aspiration is not emphasized in the Theravada and other historical schools outside of the *mahāyāna*, compassion certainly is. The 'four immeasurables' of compassion, loving-kindness, sympathetic joy, and equality are fundamental to these schools as well. Another feature often cited as distinguishing the *mahāyāna* from the *hīnayāna* is the understanding of the philosophical position of emptiness. Note, however, that this distinction is not as clear as is often portrayed, and emptiness certainly is discussed outside of the *mahāyāna*. See the discussion in chapter five.
4. Patrul Rinpoche, *Letter*, 106.
5. The fact that the enlightened mind is present from the very beginning of the path is expressed in some *mahāyāna sūtras*, and is the theme of the Tibetan *dzogchen*, *lamdre*, and *mahāmudrā* traditions. In some practice lineages, the recognition of the presence of this enlightened mind comes at the beginning of the path, and informs all subsequent practice.
6. See, for example, the beginning of chapter six of *The Words of My Perfect Teacher* (Patrul Rinpoche 1998: 137).
7. The major schools that developed in the period of the second diffusion (Tib. *phyi dar*) are detailed below. There were other schools that did not survive as independent entities into the twentieth century, such as the Bulug and Jonang, though the latter is now being revived.
8. Another tradition that has *terma* is the Bonpo's, whose teachings are historically differentiated from Buddhism, though many Bonpo consider themselves as one of the schools of Tibetan Buddhism, a situation that has been approved by the fourteenth Dalai Lama.
9. On the origins of *dzogchen*, see van Schaik 2004a, and on Jigme Lingpa see van Schaik 2004b.

10. For an introduction to the literature and practices of the Kadam school, see Jinpa 2013.
11. The history and practices of the Sakya school are detailed in Dhongthog 2016. A number of other schools developed from the Sakya tradition, including the Jonang, Bodong, and Bulug; the latter two no longer exist, but the Jonang is currently being revived, despite nearly disappearing after it was suppressed in the seventeenth century by the fifth Dalai Lama.
12. On the early development of the Kagyu school, see Jampa Thaye 1990.
13. On Tsongkhapa's life and works, see Thurman 2009.
14. See Dreyfus 2003, especially chapter seven, for an insightful account of the role of reading, memorization, and transmission in Tibetan Buddhism. See Carruthers 2008 for a classic study of medieval European practices of reading and memorization.

CHAPTER 2. A CODE OF ETHICS

1. The edicts are preserved in *The Scholars' Feast* by Pawo Tsuglag Trengwa. My translation here is from the Tibetan text in Richardson 1998: 97 (110b).
2. The edict of Senaleg, carved on a pillar that was found in Karchung, mentions spreading Buddhism through 'the whole of Tibet' and that all Tibetans 'from the nobles on down' should be able to practise. See Richardson 1985: 78–9 (ll. 33–42). The edict by Ralpachen is referred to in the colophon of a scroll in the British Library, Or.8210/S.3966: 'In the sixth month of the water tiger year, a letter was issued with the seal of the Tibetan king to be circulated throughout the prefectures of Greater Tibet with copies of this *Sutra of the Ten Virtues* for widespread recitation.'
3. *Maṇi Kambum* 1: 163b. The creation of the Tibetan law code based on the ten virtues is related in most Tibetan histories, including: *The Testimony of Ba*, the *Maṇi Kambum*, Sonam Tsemo's *Introduction to the Dharma*, and Lama Dampa's *Clear Mirror*. For English translations, see, for example, Sørensen 1994, and Pasang and Diemberger 2000.
4. See Jampa Thaye 2006: 13–23.
5. See Jampa Thaye 2006: 24–8. Jampa Thaye (24) states that 'there are eight types of pratimoksa vow: those of a lay man, lay woman, female probationer, novice monk, novice nun, monk, nun and the vow of temporary abstinence'.
6. The distinction between the greater and lesser vehicles is best understood as a way of conceptualizing the Buddhist path, rather than a description of historical schools of Buddhist practice. The historical development of the greater vehicle, and its relationship to other forms of Buddhism, is best understood through reading an overview of the development of Buddhism, such as Hirakawa 1990 or Skilton 1994. On the *mahāyāna* in particular, see Williams 2008.
7. A good traditional Tibetan explanation of these principles, in the context of the ten virtues and other fundamental practices, is to be found in *Words of My Perfect Teacher* by Patrul Rinpoche (1808–87), a nineteenth-century work written for lay Buddhists (Patrul Rinpoche 1998).
8. Most of the manucripts from the 'library cave' at Dunhuang date from before the turn of the millennium, 1000 CE; see van Schaik and Galambos 2012 for a discussion of the contents of the cave and the reasons for its sealing. Most of the

Tibetan manuscripts are now kept at the British Library in London and the Bibliothèque nationale de France in Paris. The five manuscripts of *The Ten Virtues* are: (i) IOL Tib J 606: a large folio of the sort used to copy the *Perfection of Wisdom Sutra* during the imperial period, with the complete text. (ii) Pelliot tibétain 968: a scroll, written in the handwriting style used by scribes in the imperial period; contains most of the text, missing only a torn section at the beginning, and ending with the title *A Teaching on the Ten Virtues.* (iii) Pelliot tibétain 4: *The Ten Virtues* is the seventh text on this concertina manuscript (v.1-13), alongside various prayers and offering rituals. It seems to have been recited in this ritual context. The handwriting suggests that the manuscript is from the tenth century. The beginning of the text is missing, but the end is present and has the title *An Extensive Teaching on the Ten Virtues.* (iv) Pelliot tibétain 971: a fragmentary single folio. (v) IOL Tib J 660: a complete single folio. Pelliot tibétain 4 & 660 seem to represent a version with a corrected orthography; for example, they change all *ji* to *ci* and all *thams chad* to *thams cad.*

9. The eight meditation states listed here are the four absorptions (Skt. *dhyāna*) with form, and the four formless absorptions, each representing a more refined state of consciousness. These are taught in early Buddhist texts, but often rejected in *mahāyāna sūtras* and treatises such as this one as distractions from the state of enlightenment, leading to rebirths in the god realms, but not liberation from *saṃsāra.* On these early teachings, and the twelve links of dependent origination, see Bronkhorst 2009.

CHAPTER 3. HOW TO LIVE

1. The only accounts of Atiśa's life are in Tibetan sources; most important is the biography by his disciple Dromton. Tārā is the bodhisattva representing compassionate activity, the subject of many devotional practices in *vajrayāna* Buddhism. Vikramaśīla (in modern Bihar) was one of the major Buddhist universities, alongside Nālandā.
2. This story is from the royal chronicles of Ngari (see Vitali 1996: 115–17). There was also a third prince, who does not play a major part in the narrative. The more common later story has Yeshe O being captured and ransomed, but this seems to be a myth tying Yeshe O to the invitation of Atiśa, in which he probably had no involvement.
3. An account of Nagtso's mission to bring Atiśa to Tibet, with many mythological flourishes, is discussed and partially translated in Decleer 1997.
4. For a translation of *Lamp for the Path to Enlightenment* see Sherburne 2003. On Atiśa's translation and teaching of tantric texts, see Jinpa 2008: 5–6.
5. On Buddhism during this period, see Davidson 2006.
6. Jinpa 2008: 7–8.
7. Translation from Jinpa 2008: 61.
8. See Jinpa 2014: 7–14. Reproductions of a Tibetan print of these two texts appear at the end of Chattopadhyaya 1999. However, the pages are out of order.
9. Jampa Thaye 2006: 33–6. There is also a distinction between conventional *bodhicitta* and ultimate *bodhicitta.* The former is what is discussed here, while the latter is the wisdom that perceives emptiness.
10. This way of approaching the practice of virtue can be compared to the movement of 'virtue ethics' in modern philosophy (see Keown 2005: 23–8). For an influential

text on virtue ethics see Macintyre 1981. A disconnect with virtue ethics has been raised by Paul Williams (2009), namely that the state of buddhahood, the ultimate aim of virtuous behaviour, is often said to be beyond dualistic concepts including virtue and sin. In addition, Barbara Clayton has argued that *mahāyāna* Buddhist ethics should also be compared with *dualistic* consequentialism, 'a kind of moral theory in which character is the prime concern, and the best traits of character are those which tend to lead to the best consequences' (Clayton 2009: 15).

11. Compositions by Buddhist authors usually begin with a statement of homage to one or more buddhas and teachers. Here Atiśa pays homage to his favoured deity Tārā ('conqueror' being an epithet for a buddha or bodhisattva) and to his teachers.

CHAPTER 4. TRAINING THE MIND

1. Patrul Rinpoche, *Letter*, 107. The presence of the enlightened mind in every sentient being is expressed in *mahāyāna sūtras* in the concept of the 'buddha nature' (a loose translation of *tathāgatāgarbha*). According to scriptures such as the *Śrīmālādevī sūtra*, the *tathāgatāgarbha* is identical with the *dharmakāya*, the true nature of reality. The difference is only in the presence or absence of that which obscures it, i.e. the conceptual and emotional factors of an ordinary sentient being. These ideas were important in China in the early development of the Zen tradition, and also informed much tantric practice, including the contemplative tradition of *dzogchen*, which Patrul Rinpoche is invoking in this verse.
2. On Geshe Chekawa's *Seven Points of Mind Training* see Jinpa 2006: 9–13, and Sweet 1996: 249–50. The seven points of mind training are often taught through the commentary of Gyalse Thogme Zangpo (1295–1369), who was also the author of a popular commentary on *The Way of the Bodhisattva* and an influential verse summary of the bodhisattva path, *Thirty-Seven Practices of a Buddha's Child.*
3. Thubten Jinpa (2006: 649, n1010) suggests that the teaching of parting from the four attachments might have originated with Dragpa Gyaltsen rather than Sachen Kunga Nyingpo. This is possible, as the four basic lines do not appear among Sachen's work, only in an anonymous preface to Dragpa Gyaltsen's text (*Collected Works of Sakya*, 9: 594). Furthermore, another practice manual on the four lines by Dragpa Gyaltsen's student Nupa Rigzin Dragpa appears to state that the original teaching came from Dragpa Gyaltsen (see Jinpa 2006: 528). The question cannot be easily resolved from biographical sources, as neither the biography of Sachen by Dragpa Gyaltsen, nor the biography of Dragpa Gyaltsen by Sakya Paṇḍita mentions the four lines, though the latter does mention Sachen's vision of Mañjuśrī which is identified as the origin of the four lines in the anonymous preface and elsewhere (*Collected Works of Sakya*, 10: 578).
4. Another brief practice manual, drawn from the works of Nupa Rigzin Dragpa and Sakya Paṇḍita, is collected in the *Treasury of Oral Instructions*, 18: 128–30 (not translated in Jinpa 2006).
5. According to the colophon, Ngorchen Kunga Zangpo's text was published from the notes of his student Kunga Legpa, which were personally approved by Ngorchen. Thubten Jinpa (2006: 541) attributes the text to Kunga Legpa, but its authorship is traditionally attributed to Ngorchen. It is in fact the case that many texts in the Tibetan Buddhist tradition were published based on notes taken by students from oral teachings; see Cabezon 2001.

6. On the life and works of Gorampa, see Dhongthog 2016. For more on the political events mentioned here, see van Schaik 2011. A further four volumes have been added to the thirteen volumes of Gorampa's collected works, but these actually contain works by some of his most eminent students.
7. The eight preoccupations are found in Nāgārjuna's *Letter to a Friend*, which is also widely taught in Tibetan Buddhism as a concise summation of the vehicle of the perfections.
8. The simile of the turtle is found in the *Majjima Nikaya* (in Pali), and in Matṛceṭa's hymn to the Buddha *Śatapañcaśatka* (in Sanskrit).
9. The four contemplations up to this point are often grouped together in other texts, as Gorampa points out. Together they are known as 'the four thoughts that turn the mind to *dharma*'.
10. Chapter 8, verse 96 of *The Way of the Bodhisattva*, translated in Crosby and Skilton 1996: 96.
11. It is often explained that the practice of sending and taking will not actually bring the suffering of all beings upon one's head; it is intended as an imaginative contemplation to transform one's character.
12. In the Sakya teaching tradition, the inner *madhyamaka* is taught in the context of the practices known as *korde yerme*, 'the inseparability of *saṃsāra* and *nirvāṇa*', which as part of the introductory practices of the *lamdre* are not promulgated outside of the teacher-student relationship.
13. There is a guru yoga mind-training text derived from Zhonnu Gyalchog; see Jinpa 2006: 199–202.
14. The word translated as 'mindfulness' here, *dran pa*, also means 'to remember'.
15. In the first opening verse, Gorampa pays homage to the Buddha Śākyamuni and the two bodhisattvas, Avalokiteśvara and Mañjuśrī, and finally to Sachen Kunga Nyingpo, the originator of the basic verse of 'parting from the four attachments'. In the second, he pays homage to the patron who requested this teaching, who is mentioned by name at the end of the text.
16. The *Ornament of Realization* is written on the schema of the eight realizations (*abhisamaya*), which are: (i) knowledge of all aspects; (ii) knowledge of the path; (iii) knowledge of the basis; (iv) application of all aspects; (v) application at peak level; (vi) progressive application; (vii) instantaneous application; and (viii) the *dharmakāya*.
17. The four errors are the erroneous beliefs that persons and phenomena are: (i) pure, (ii) enjoyable, (iii) permanent, and (iv) possess an inherent self or nature.
18. These practices are known as 'the seven points of mind training' and are discussed in the text of that name by Geshe Chekawa and its later commentaries. See the introduction to this chapter.
19. The three brothers were all disciples of Dromton: Putowa Rinchen Sel, Chengawa Tsultrim Bar, and Puchungwa Zhonnu Gyaltsan. Gyalse Chodzongpa, also known as Gyalse Thogme Zangpo (1295–1369), was a Sakya teacher, who wrote *A Commentary on the Seven-Point Mind-training* as well as the equally popular *Thirty-Seven Practices of a Buddha's Child*. His disciples included Rendawa Zhonnu Lodro (1349–1412), one of the principal teachers of Tsongkhapa (1357–1419), founder of the Gelug school, and Sangye Pel (1339–1420), one of the teachers of Ngorchen Kunga Zango (1382–1456), the first abbot of the Ngor branch of the Sakya school, who also wrote a commentary on *Parting from the Four Attachments*. The other teacher mentioned here, Zhonnu Gyalchog (four-

teenth century), is considered to have transmitted both Kadam and Sakya lineages of mind training (he studied with another of Thogme Zangpo's students) and is best known as the compiler of a major collection of mind-training texts.

20. The eight freedoms are freedom from being born in the hell realms, as a hungry ghost, as an animal, in a place where the *dharma* will not be encountered, as a god, as a person with erroneous views, in a world where no buddha has appeared, or lacking the sensory and mental faculties required to practise the *dharma*. The ten endowments are: to be born as a human being; where the *dharma* can be found; with all five senses; not having committed serious non-virtuous activities; having confidence in the buddha, *dharma* and *sangha*; and also to be born in a world where a buddha has appeared; has taught the *dharma*; where the *dharma* has flourished; and there are students practising the *dharma*; and finally where one has access to a qualified teacher.
21. The three realms of *saṃsāra* are the realms of desire, form, and formlessness. The realm of desire encompasses most of samsaric existence, including gods, demigods, humans, animals, hungry ghosts, and dwellers in hell. The realms of form and formlessness correspond to increasingly abstract meditative absorptions, which are nevertheless temporary and do not lead to freedom from *saṃsāra*.
22. It might seem a contradiction that the practices here, which are aimed at developing the awakening mind, must be preceded by the preliminary practice of generating the awakening mind. However, these preliminaries are only brief prayers, the main function of reciting them being to establish the context of the practice as Buddhist (taking refuge) and *mahāyāna* (generating the awakening mind). Thus the preliminary practice of generating the awakening mind does not entail the full development of the awakening mind.
23. The three spheres are the three concepts of the agent of an action, the act itself, and the object or beneficiary of the action.
24. The month of Mindrug (*smin drug*, Skt. *kārtikka*), from the calendrical system of the *Wheel of Time Tantra*, corresponds to October–November. The patron Ralo Dorje, and the subsequent work written for him that Gorampa refers to here, have not been identified.

CHAPTER 5. THE NATURE OF THINGS

1. This simplified account of the *abhidharma* is based on Hirakawa 1990. There were a great many differences in interpretation of the nature of *dharmas* among the various movements within *abhidharma* philosophy. For instance, dependent origination was also considered to be an unconditioned *dharma* in some *abhidharma* schools of thought (Hirakawa 1990: 148).
2. *Root Verses on the Madhyamaka*, chapter 24, verses 18–19.
3. Some modern Western scholars present Nāgārjuna as negating all phenomenal existence, making him a nihilist (e.g. Bronkhorst 2009: 135–52). This would be plausible if Nāgārjuna's works equated *dharmas* with phenomena, but they do not. In works such as the *Root Verses on the Madhyamaka*, the concept of *dharmas* as the basis for the phenomenal world is negated, and replaced by the model of dependent origination. After the idea of independently existing *dharmas* is negated, phenomena continue, characterized instead as arising dependently. Thus nihilism seems a misleading characterization of this position; a more

accurate Western philosophical term for Nāgārjuna's negative arguments might be 'anti-foundationalism'.

4. *Exposition of Bodhicitta*, verse 67.
5. *Dispelling Disputes*, verse 29.
6. The same is true of his contemporary Śāntideva's discussion of *madhyamaka* in the ninth chapter of *The Way of the Bodhisattva*.
7. See van Schaik 2015.
8. *Questions of Milinda*, book 2, chapter 1 (translation from Rhys Davids 1890: 43–4).
9. *Entering the Madhyamaka*, chapter 6, verse 151.
10. *Entering the Madhyamaka*, chapter 6, verse 158.
11. *Entering the Madhyamaka*, chapter 6, verse 9. Translation (and other verses from *Entering the Madhyamaka* below) based on Huntington 1989. In later verses on this same argument, Candrakīrti addresses a position he attributes to the Saṃkhya school, that, though various qualities such as shape and colour are different in the seed and the sprout, the intrinsic nature is the same. Candrakīrti counters this by employing arguments against the idea of an intrinsic nature existing separately from form.
12. *Entering the Madhyamaka*, chapter 6, verse 99.
13. In the *madhyamaka* tradition of the Gelug school, *prāsaṅgika* is considered absolutely superior to *svātantrika*, and the distinction between the two is presented as irreconcilable. Mipham Gyatso, whose *madhyamaka* writings show the influence of Gorampa, included aspects of *svātantrika* in his presentation of *madhyamaka*, and argued against the denigration of *svātantrika* by Tsongkhapa and other Gelug writers. See Petit 2002.
14. In the simplest terms, Gorampa criticized Dolpopa for not negating emptiness itself, and Tsongkhapa for not accepting that the four extremes are negated simultaneously in the ultimate truth. The complete text of *Distinguishing the View* is translated in Cabezon and Dargyay 2007. On the issues in question between Gorampa and Tsongkhapa, see also Thakchoe 2007. On Dolpopa and his works, see Stearns 1999. The 'empty of other' interpretation of *madhyamaka* was also favoured by the Sakya scholar Shakya Chogden (1428–1507).
15. Thus it is not necessary to claim (as some have done when interpreting Gorampa and other *madhyamaka* writers) that one can negate the validity of all conceptual thought using only the conceptual arguments of the *madhyamaka* that refute existence and non-existence. In any case, such a claim assumes that all language is founded on the concept of independent existence, which is far from obvious and probably a fallacy. See for example Kassor 2011: 126–7.
16. In modern scholarship, it is now generally accepted that the idea of the emptiness of *dharmas* had already been developed in *abhidharma* texts of the Sarvāstivāda school (Bronkhorst 2012: 490–1).
17. Here, the 'Mind Only school' refers to the texts and practices of the *yogācāra*, also known as *cittamātra* (Sanskrit for 'mind only'), which developed in India in the fourth and fifth centuries CE based on *sūtras* such as the *Sutra of Unravelling the Knot* and the works of Vasubandhu and Asaṅga. For a survey of *yogācāra*, see Williams 2008.
18. The two schools of the hearers that Gorampa refers to here are the Vaibhāṣika and Sautrāntika. Historically, these appear to have been movements within the Sarvāstivāda tradition. The Vaibhāṣika was based in Kashmir, and was a relatively

conservative commentarial tradition on *abhidharma*. The Sautrāntika were based in Gandhara and put forward positions that were sometimes critical of previous *abhidharma* philosophy. See Hirakawa 1990: 135–8. In the Tibetan Buddhist tradition, the two schools are remembered only through a simplified version of their philosophical views: the Vaibhāṣika are said to have asserted the existence of indivisible constituents of matter, while the Sautrāntikas asserted the existence of indivisible moments of consciousness.

19. Gorampa's basic point here is that *madhyamaka* philosophers should not be producing explanations about the nature of causality or any other aspect of conventional experience. He follows Candrakīrti in asserting that conventional truth can be accepted simply in terms of ordinary experience. Elsewhere in *Distinguishing the View* Gorampa goes into more detail in his argument against Tsongkhapa's theory of causation involving 'destruction as a *dharma*'.
20. Elsewhere in *Distinguishing the View*, Gorampa explicitly argues against Tsongkhapa's view that in the case of multiple and different perceptions of a single object, both perceived objects (e.g. water, blood, and pus) must be simultaneously present.
21. Conceptualization (Tib. *rtogs pa*) is the difference between the approximate ultimate and the definitive ultimate truth, and in this text Gorampa repeatedly defines conceptualization as that which identifies words with their referents. This definition, though based on Indian philosophical terms, may be compared to de Saussure's concept of a sign as being composed of a signifier (the sound) and a signified (the general idea associated with that sound). For Gorampa and the tradition of Tibetan scholasticism to which he belonged, conceptualization consists of apprehending the combination of the word or sound (Tib. *sgra*) and its general meaning (Tib. *don*). See also Cabezon and Dargyay 2007: 331 n379: 'Instead of seeing its referent clearly, as does direct perception (*mngon sum*), conceptual thought is an erroneous (*'khrul pa*) form of consciousness that mixes up the word and its meaning (the generic image = *don spyi*).'
22. In answering these two objections, Gorampa argues that logical rules, such as the rule that one cannot deny both existence and nonexistence to the same object, apply to conventional truth but not to ultimate truth. At the level of ultimate truth the four extremes of existence, nonexistence, both, and neither are simultaneously denied.
23. In this passage Gorampa states that only the definitive (i.e. non-conceptual) realization of the emptiness of the four extremes can be called the definitive ultimate truth. Cabezon and Dargyay (2007: 217) interpret this passage as saying that the definitive realizations of all forms of emptiness are equivalent to the definitive ultimate truth; however, this would contradict Gorampa's statements elsewhere in the text that the followers of the *hīnayāna* do not realize the definitive ultimate truth.
24. In this paragraph, Gorampa states that the phrase 'grasping at the true existence of *dharmas*' applies not only to grasping at existence (the first of the four extremes) but also grasping at nonexistence (the second extreme), a combination of both (the third extreme), or an assertion that neither are true (the fourth extreme).
25. The two obscurations refer to a division of the factors that obscure the innate presence of the enlightened mind into (i) obscuration by emotional afflictions (Skt. *kleśa*) and (ii) obscuration by cognitive factors (Skt. *jñeya*). In this para-

graph, Gorampa explains his position that grasping at the true existence of *dharmas* is a cognitive obscuration, while grasping at the true existence of the person is obscuration by the afflictions. Moreover, he argues that obscuration by the afflictions actually derives from cognitive obscuration, as grasping at the true existence of the person derives from grasping at the true existence of *dharmas*. Elsewhere in *Distinguishing the View*, he argues explicitly against Tsongkhapa's argument that both kinds of grasping at true existence are forms of obscuration by the afflictions.

26. Gorampa's point in this section is a subtle one, and is perhaps not immediately clear. He states in this first paragraph that the hearers *claim* that understanding the lack of personal self based on the deconstruction of the person into aggregates is sufficient to achieve enlightenment, and that they do not believe that it is also necessary to understand that the aggregates themselves lack true existence. However, Gorampa goes on to argue that, whatever they might say about the matter, if they are to overcome self-clinging the hearers *must* in fact understand that the aggregates lack true existence. That is to say, the hearers not only understand (i) the lack of true existence of the self, which is *based on* the aggregates, but also (ii) the lack of true existence of *dharmas*, which refutes the true existence of the aggregates themselves. The translation in Cabezon and Dargyay (2007: 221) obscures this point by making it seem that Gorampa states in the first paragraph that the hearers do not understand the aggregates as empty of true existence, and then proceeds to contradict himself a few paragraphs later.
27. The path of seeing is one of the five paths, one of the ways of understanding the stages of spiritual progress; specifically, the path of seeing is the point at which one first glimpses the true state of reality.
28. The 'unparalleled lord of the *dharma*' referred to by Goramapa here is his own teacher, Rongton Sheja Kunrig, also known as Rongtonpa (1367–1449). It is an interesting, but not unusual, example of a Tibetan scholar criticizing the interpretations of his own teacher.
29. The two buddha bodies are the *dharmakāya* and the *rūpakāya*, representing, respectively, the unconditioned state of enlightenment, and its manifestation in the world in order to save sentient beings. Gorampa has probably decided not to discuss the topic here as it does not touch on the debates regarding the *madhyamaka* that are the topic of this text. A discussion of the two bodies can be found in Candrakīrti's *Entering the Madhyamaka*.

CHAPTER 6. THE PATH

1. This summary of the four types of tantra is based on Sonam Tsemo's text, though it is not in the chapters translated here. The system of four classes of tantra was adopted by most Tibetan interpreters of the tantras, apart from those of the Nyingma school, who distinguished six classes of tantra as part of a division of the whole of the Buddhist path into nine vehicles (see Dalton 2005).
2. According to Jetsun Dragpa Gyaltsen in *Dispelling Error*, it is the vase initiation (generally only found in yoga and supreme yoga tantra initiations) that entails a commitment to the *vidyādhara* vows. Dragpa Gyaltsen's enumeration of fourteen fundamental vows and eight branch vows in this work (derived from the *Hevajra Tantra* tradition) has become the standard interpretation followed in the Sakya

and Gelug school, and by most in the Kagyu school. In the Nyingma school a set of three fundamental vows and twenty-five branch vows is followed (derived from the tradition of the *Guhyagarbha Tantra*); see van Schaik 2010.

3. The mantra *oṃ maṇi padme hūṃ* is often explained in Western publications as referring to 'the jewel in the lotus', and as a tantric sexual metaphor. A much more plausible explanation is that the words *maṇi padme* refer to a popular form of Avalokiteśvara, who is depicted holding both a jewel and a lotus. The syllables *oṃ* and *hūṃ* on the other hand are common in mantras and have no literal meaning.
4. The four superiorities indicate the superiority of the vehicle of the secret mantra over the vehicle of the perfections and are detailed later in the text, in the fourth main section. They are: (i) being without confusion regarding the view of realization; (ii) having many methods of attaining the result; (iii) attaining enlightenment without difficulties; and (iv) intended for those of sharp faculties because the result is swiftly obtained.
5. Here Sonam Tsemo is describing the twelve links of dependent origination (Skt. *pratītyasamutpāda*), though the order is not the usual one.
6. The ten stages (Skt. *bhūmi*) are the most common scheme for the gradual enlightenment of a bodhisattva. Here Sonam Tsemo links the phases of practice outlined in the *Ornament of the Sutras* with the ten stages. The 'stage achieved through faith' is a preparatory stage of practice that precedes the ten stages proper. Another scheme found in some *vajrayāna* texts extends the sequence to thirteen stages, and elsewhere in this text, when discussing the *vajrayāna*, Sonam Tsemo mentions a thirteenth stage.
7. The *Hevajra Tantra* goes on to associate a deity with each of the six senses (sight, hearing, smell, taste, touch, and consciousness).

CHAPTER 7. PRAYER

1. On the artistic representation of the elders / *arhats* in Tibet, see Linrothe 2004; in China, see de Visser 1923.
2. On the *Aspirational Prayer of Samantabhadra* (Skt. *Samantabhadra-praṇidhāna*), see Osto 2010).
3. On the practice of the confession ritual and other rituals in Tibetan monasteries, see Dreyfus 2003: 44–7.
4. The act of rejoicing is described at length in the thirty-third chapter of the *Perfection of Wisdom in Ten Thousand Verses*. See Conze 1990 [1975]: 269–82.
5. This *dhāraṇī* is in Sanskrit but is rendered here in something closer to the Tibetan pronunciation of the Sanskrit, to give a sense of how it is recited.
6. A note, probably by Jamyang Kyentse Wangpo, between the previous two lines states: 'I wonder if something is missing between the above two lines?'
7. These four verses in praise of all the buddhas are the beginning of the *Aspirational Prayer of Excellent Conduct*.
8. Dharmatāra is not one of the sixteen *arhats*, but is usually associated with them. He is depicted travelling with books and other materials on his back. In China he is associated with Buddhist pilgrims such as Xuanzang. Like the four great kings in the next verse, he is considered an attendant and protector of the sixteen *arhats*.
9. These are verses 5–7 of the *Aspirational Prayer of Excellent Conduct*.

CHAPTER 8. THE LIFE OF A MASTER

1. A major biography was written by Jamgon Kongtrul Lodro Taye, and has been translated by Akester 2012.
2. At the request of Khyentse Wangpo, Jamgon Kongtrul also edited and published further collections, including the *Treasury of Oral Transmissions* and the *Treasury of Kagyu Mantra*. Later, Khyentse's student Loter Wangpo (1847–1914) edited and published another major collection based on Khyentse's finds, the *Compendium of Sādhanas*.
3. Another formulation of these three activities is composition, teaching, and debate.
4. For a traditional account of different types of treasure, see Tulku Thondup 2005. On the history of *terma*, see Davidson 2006, chapter six.
5. The concept of 'emanation' (*sprul pa*) differs from that of 'rebirth' (*yang srid*). One of these differences is that one person can, after death, give rise to more than one emanation.
6. The deities that Khyentse Wangpo mentions seeing in his earliest memories are the six-armed form of Mahākāla and another *dharma* protector, Ekajaṭi.
7. The 'great island of teachings that ripen and liberate' is the Nyingma monastery of Mindroling, which was very active in central Tibet (U) in the eighteenth century, in the time of the brothers Lochen Dharmashri and Terdag Lingpa. The *Heart Essence of the Vidyādharas* is a *terma* revealed by the latter. The three kinds of vow that Khyentse Wangpo received here are the monastic vows, the bodhisattva vow, and the *vidyādhara* vows of higher tantric initiations (on which, see chapters two, four and six).
8. In this verse Khyentse Wangpo lists the main schools in which he received instruction; along with Kadam and Sakya, there are four Kagyu schools, Drikung, Taklung, Karma (here named for its main monastery, Tsurpu), and Drugpa. These are all 'new schools' from the second diffusion of Buddhism in Tibet, but Khyentse Wangpo also mentions the old school (Nyingma) here, and lists two Nyingma tantras, the *Magical Net* and *Secret Matrix*.
9. The 'great *stūpa*' mentioned here is the main *stūpa* at Lhundrupteng, the largest Sakya monastery in Derge, which was destroyed during the Cultural Revolution, and has since been rebuilt.
10. The political troubles mentioned here are discussed in detail in the autobiography of Jamgon Kongtrul; see the translation by Jamgon Kongtrul 2003: 127–36. See also Tsering 1985.
11. In this verse Khyentse Wangpo mentions his success in converting practitioners of Bon, the non-Buddhist religion of Tibet, to Buddhism.
12. The 'three spheres of a teacher's activity' are the traditional aspects of the outer biography, renunciation, study, and good works.
13. The eight chariots are (i) Nyingma, (ii) Kadam, (iii) Sakya, (iv) Marpa Kagyu, (v) Shangpa Kagyu, (vi) the six yogas of the *Wheel of Time*, (vii) Pacification and Cutting, and (viii) Orgyenpa's deity yoga of three *vajras*. The meditative practices of pacification (*zhi byed*) and cutting (*gcod*) derive from the Indian teacher Dampa Sangye, who was active in Tibet in the twelfth century. The six yogas derive from the *Wheel of Time Tantra*, translated into Tibetan in the eleventh century, and were the speciality of the Jonang school. 'The deity yoga of the three vajras' is related to the six yogas of the *Wheel of Time*, and was brought to Tibet

from Oḍḍiyāna by Orgyenpa Rinchenpal in the thirteenth century. Both lineages were very rare by the nineteenth century. See Stearns 2001: 4–7.

14. Here 'the Great Orgyen' is an honorific name for Padmasambhava, Pema Totreng Tsel is a wrathful form of Padmasambhava, and Vajrakīlaya is a wrathful deity from the Nyingma and Sakya practice lineages. The prophecies mentioned here are those found in various *terma* texts that were identified by Jamyang Khyentse Wangpo or his disciples as references to his life.
15. Mañjuśjrīmitra, who probably lived in the eighth century, was the author of tantric commentaries, *sādhanas*, and at least one early *dzogchen* text.
16. *The Heart Mirror of Vajrasattva* is one of the seventeen tantras of the *dzogchen* 'Heart Essence' tradition.
17. Tangtong Gyalpo (1385–1464) was a fifteenth-century master associated with Kagyu and Nyingma schools, who is also famous for building iron bridges (hence his nickname Chagzampa, 'Iron Bridge') and founding Tibet's tradition of religious theatre. In this context 'the Heart Essence' refers to the highest teachings and practices of *dzogchen.*
18. The seven transmissions are the different routes through which teachings have been received and passed down in the Nyingma school. They include scriptural collections transmitted in the usual way, known as *kama* (Tib. *bka' ma*), and hidden treasures (*gter ma*). Similar to, but distinct from treasures, are 'pure visions' (*dag snang*), in which teachings are received in a visionary state, but are not considered to be rediscovered.
19. These verses in praise of Jamgon Kongtrul should perhaps belong in the outer biography, but may be included here as they mention the compilation of the *Treasury of Precious Terma,* following on from the verses about the seven transmissions above.
20. Vajraghaṇṭapa (usually known as Ghaṇṭapa) is one of the legendary *mahasiddhas* or 'great adepts' of India. Anantamukhamati is a reconstructed Sanskrit name based on the Tibetan *sgo mtha' yas pa'i blo gros;* Matthew Akester (2012, 181n7) translates the name as Pratihārāmati, and suggests that this could be an alternative name for the sixth-century scholar Sthiramati. Vanaratna (1384–1468) was a Bengali specialist in the *Wheel of Time,* one of the last known Indian Buddhist *paṇḍitas* to visit Tibet.
21. These are two Tibetan emperors, Tri Song Detsen (r.742–c.800) and Chogdrup Gyalpo, who ruled as Tri De Songtsen (r.800–815). Guru Chowang (1212–70) was one of the early treasure revealers. Ngari Paṇḍita (1487–1542) was a scholar and treasure revealer in the Nyingma school. See the note above on Tangtong Gyalpo. Lhatsun Namkai Jigme (1597–1653) was a meditator and teacher in the *dzogchen* 'Heart Essence' tradition.
22. I have not been able to identify Khetsun Zangpo (the well-known Nyingma lama of that name was not born until 1920). Jigme Trinley Ozer (1745–1821) was the first Dodrupchen Rinpoche. Prince Damzin is Murub Tsenpo, one of the sons of the emperor Tri Song Detsen. The person who requested this autobiography, Jigme Tenpai Nyima, the third Dodrupchen Rinpoche (1865–1926), was a student of Jamyang Khyentse Wangpo, Jamgon Kongtrul, and several Nyingma masters of the period, including Patrul Rinpoche.

BIBLIOGRAPHY

Sanskrit and Tibetan Texts

Aspirational Prayer of Samantabhadra
Skt. *Samantabhadracārya-praṇidhāna*
Tib. *Kun tu bzang po'i spyod pa'i smon lam*

Awakening of Vairocana
Skt. *Vairocana-abhisaṃbodhi-sūtra*
Tib. *Rnam par snang mdzad mngon par byang chub pa*

Cakrasaṃvara Tantra
Skt. *Cakrasaṃvara-tantra*
Tib. *'Khor lo bde mchog gi rgyud*

Clear Mirror, Lama Dampa
Tib. *Rgyal rabs gsal ba'i me long*

Clouds of Offerings Dhāraṇī
Skt. *Pūjāmegha-dhāraṇī*
Tib. *Mchod pa'i sprin gyi gzungs*

Collected Works of Sakya
Tib. *Sa skya bka' 'bum*

Commentary on Logic, Dharmakīrti
Skt. *Pramāṇvārttika*
Tib. *Tshad ma rnam 'grel*

Compendium of Tantras, ed. Loter Wangpo
Tib. *Rgyud sde kun 'dus*

Dispelling Disputes, Nāgārjuna
Skt. *Vigrahavyāvartanā*
Tib. *Rtsod pa bzlog pa'i tshig le'ur byas pa*

Dispelling Error: A Commentary on the Fourteen Root Downfalls, Dragpa Gyaltsen
Tib. *Rtsa ba'i ltung ba bcu bzhi pa'i 'grel pa gsal byed 'khrul spyong*

Distinguishing the Middle and the Extremes, Asaṅga
Skt. *Madhyāntavibhāga-kārikā*
Tib. *Dbus mtha' rnam byed*

Eight Verses of Mind Training, Langri Tangpa
Tib. *Blo sbyong tshigs rkang brgyad ma*

Entering the Madhyamaka, Candrakīrti
Skt. *Madhyamakāvatāra*
Tib. *Dbu ma la 'jug pa*

Entrance to the Two Truths, Nāgārjuna
Skt. *Satyadvayāvatāra*
Tib. *Bden gnyis la 'jug pa*

Exposition of Bodhicitta, Nāgārjuna
Skt. *Bodhicittavivarana*
Tib. *Byang chub sems dpa'i 'grel pa*

Extensive Play Sutra
Skt. *Lalitavistara-sūtra*
Tib. *Rgya cher rol pa'i mdo*

Five Commitments
Tib. *Dam tshig lnga*

Flower Garland Sutra
Skt. *Avataṃsaka-sūtra*
Tib. *Me tog rna rgyan phal mo che'i mdo*

Heart Essence of the Vidyādharas
Tib. *Rig 'dzin snying thig*

Heart Mirror of Vajrasattva
Tib. *Rdo rje sems dpa'i snying gi me long*

Hevajra Tantra
Skt. *Hevajra-tantra*
Tib. *Kye rdo rje'i rgyud / Brtag gnyis*

Illumination of the Madhyamaka, Kamalaśīla
Skt. *Madhyamakāloka*
Tib. *Dbu ma'i snang ba*

Introduction to the Dharma, Sonam Tsemo
Tib. *Chos la 'jug pa'i sgo*

Jewel Garland of the Bodhisattva, Atiśa
Tib. *Byang chub sems dpa'i nor bu'i phreng ba*

Jewel Garland of the Middle Way, Nāgārjuna
Skt. *Madhyamaka-ratnāvali*
Tib. *Dbu ma rin chen phreng ba*

Kiss Tantra
Tib. *Kun tu kha sbyor rgyud*

Lamp for the Path to Enlightenment, Atiśa
Tib. *Byang chub lam kyi sgron me*

Later Secret Assembly Tantra
Skt. *Guhyasamāja-uttaratantra*
Tib. *Gsang ba 'dus pa'i rgyud phyi ma*

Letter to a Disciple, Candragomin
Skt. *Śiṣyalekha*
Tib. *Slob ma la spring pa*

Letter to a Friend, Nāgārjuna
Skt. *Suhṛllekha*
Tib. *Bshes pa'i spring yig*

Magical Net Tantra
Skt. *Māyājāla*
Tib. *Sgyu 'phrul dra ba'i rgyud*

Maṇi Kambum
Tib. *Ma ṇi bka' 'bum*

Mission to Lanka Sutra
Skt. *Laṅkāvatāra-sūtra*
Tib. *Lang kar gshegs pa'i mdo*

Ornament of the Madhyamaka, Śāntarakṣita
Skt. *Madhyamakālaṃkāra*
Tib. *Dbu ma'i rgyan*

Ornament of Realization, Asaṅga
Skt. *Abhisamayālaṃkāra*
Tib. *Mgon rtogs rgyan*

Ornament of the Sutras, Asaṅga
Skt. *(Mahāyāna) Sutrālaṃkāra*
Tib. *(Theg pa chen po'i) mdo sde rgyan*

Parting from the Four Attachments, Sachen Kunga Nyingpo
Tib. *Zhen pa bzhi bral*

Perfection of Wisdom Sutra(s)
Skt. *Prajñāpāramitā-sūtra*
Tib. *Pha rol tu phyin pa'i mdo*

Perfection of Wisdom in Twenty-Five Thousand Lines
Skt. *Pañcaviṃśatisāhasrikā-prajñāpāramitā-sūtra*
Tib. *Shes rab kyi pha rol tu phyin pa stong phrag nyi shu lnga pa*

Perfection of Wisdom in One Hundred Thousand Lines
Skt. *Śatasāhasrikā-prajñāpāramitā-sūtra*
Tib. *Shes rab kyi pha rol tu phyin pa stong phrag brgya pa*

Praise for the Space of Reality, Nāgārjuna
Skt. *Dharmadhātustava*
Tib. *Chos kyi dbyings su bstod pa*

Questions of Milinda, anon.
Pali: *Milindapanha*

Rain of Wisdom: The Guru Yoga of the Three Buddha Bodies
Tib. *Sku gsum bla ma'i rnal 'byor ye shes char 'bebs*

Root Verses on the Madhyamaka, Nāgārjuna
Skt. *Mūlamadhyamaka-kārikā*
Tib. *Dbu ma rta ba'i tshig le'u byas pa*

Scholars' Feast, Pawo Tsuglag Trengwa
Tib. *Mkhas pa'i dga' ston*

Secret Assembly Tantra
Skt. *Guhyasamāja-tantra*
Tib. *Gsang ba 'dus pa'i rgyud*

Secret Matrix Tantra
Skt. *Guhyagarbha-tantra*
Tib. *Gsang ba snying po'i rgyud*

Secret Treasury
Tib. *Gsang ba'i mdzod*

Seven Points of Mind Training, Geshe Chekawa
Tib. *Blo sbyong don bdun ma*

Sixty Reasons, Nāgārjuna
Skt. *Yuktiṣāṣṭika-kārikā*
Tib. *Rigs pa drug cu pa*

Summation of the Perfection of Wisdom
Skt. *Prajñāpāramitā-sañcayagātha-sūtra*

Supreme Continuum, Asaṅga
Skt. *Uttaratantra-śāstra*
Tib. *Rgyud bla ma*

Sutra of the Questions of the Bodhisattva Aśvaghoṣa
Tib. *Rta skad byang chub sems dpas zhus pa'i mdo*

Sutra of the Questions of Kaśyapa
Skt. *Kaśyapaparivarta*
Tib. *'Od srung gi zhus pa'i mdo*

Sutra of Unravelling the Knot
Skt. *Saṃdhinirmocana-sūtra*
Tib. *Dgongs pa nges 'grel gi mdo*

Ten Stages Sutra
Skt. *Daśabhūmika-sūtra*
Tib. *Sa bcu pa'i mdo*

Testimony of Ba, The
Tib. *Dba' bzhed*

Thirty-Seven Practices of a Buddha's Child, Gyalse Togme Zangpo
Tib. *Rgyal ba'i sras kyi lag len sum cu so bdun ma*

Treasury of Oral Instructions, ed. Jamgon Kongtrul Lodro Taye
Tib. *Gdams ngag mdzod*

Treasury of Precious Terma, ed. Jamgon Kongtrul Lodro Taye
Tib. *Rin chen gter mdzod*

Vajra Pinnacle
Skt. *Vajraśekhara-tantra*
Tib. *Rdo rje rtse mo'i rgyud*

Vajra Tent Tantra
Skt. *Vajrapañjara-tantra*
Tib. *Rdo rje gur gyi rgyud*

Way of the Bodhisattva, The, Śāntideva
Skt. *Bodhisattvacaryāvatāra*
Tib. *Byang chub sems dpa'i spyod pa la 'jug pa*

Wheel of Time Tantra
Skt. *Kālacakra-tantra*
Tib. *Dus pa'i 'khor lo'i rgyud*

Wondrous Sayings, ed. Jamgon Kongtrul Lodro Taye
Tib. *Legs bshad rmad byung*

Words of My Perfect Teacher, Patrul Rinpoche
Tib. *Kun bzang bla ma'i zhal lung*

General Bibliography

Akester, Matthew. 2012. *The Life of Jamyang Khyentse Wangpo*. New Delhi: Shechen.

Bronkhorst, Johannes. 2009. *Buddhist Teaching in India*. Boston: Wisdom Publications.

— 2012. 'Reflections on the Origins of Mahāyāna'. *Séptimo Centenario de los Estudios Orientales en Salamanca*. Salamanca: Ediciones Universidad de Salamanca. 489–502.

Cabezon, Jose. 2001. 'Authorship and Literary Production in Classical Buddhist Tibet'. In *Changing Minds: Contribution to the Study of Buddhism and Tibet*, ed. Guy Newland. Boston: Snow Lion Publications. 233–64.

Cabezon, Jose and Geshe Lobsang Dargyay. 2007. *Freedom from Extremes: Gorampa's Distinguishing the Views and the Polemics of Emptiness*. Boston: Wisdom Publications.

Carruthers, Mary. 2008. *The Book of Memory: A Study of Memory in Medieval Culture*. 2nd ed. Cambridge: Cambridge University Press.

Chattopadhyaya, Alak. 1999 [1967]. *Atīśa and Tibet*. New Delhi: Motilal Banarsidass.

Clayton, Barbara. 2009. 'Śāntideva, Virtue, and Consequentialism'. In *Destroying Mara Forever: Buddhist Ethics Essays in Honour of Damien Keown*. Ithaca: Snow Lion Publications. 15–30.

Conze, Edward. 1990 [1975]. *The Large Sutra on Perfect Wisdom*. New Delhi: Motilal Banarsidass.

Crosby, Kate and Andrew Skilton. 1996. *The Bodhicaryāvatāra: A Guide to the Buddhist Path to Awakening*. Oxford: Oxford University Press.

Dalton, Jacob. 2005. 'A Crisis of Doxography: How Tibetans Organized Tantra during the 8th-12th Centuries'. In *Journal of the International Association of Buddhist Studies* 28.1: 115–81.

Davidson, Ronald. 2006. *Tibetan Renaissance: Tantric Buddhism in the Rebirth of Tibetan Culture*. New York: Columbia University Press.

Decleer, Hubert. 1997. 'Atisha's Journey to Tibet'. In Donald S. Lopez (ed.), *Religions of Tibet in Practice*. Princeton, NJ: Princeton University Press. 157–77.

Dhongthog Rinpoche. 2016. *The Sakya School of Tibetan Buddhism*. Trans. and ed. by Sam van Schaik. Boston: Wisdom Publications.

Dreyfus, Georges. 2003. *The Sound of Two Hands Clapping: The Education of a Buddhist Monk*. Berkeley: University of California Press.

Hirakawa Akira. 1990. *A History of Indian Buddhism from Śākyamuni to Early Mahāyāna*. Trans. and ed. by Paul Groner. Honolulu: University of Hawai'i Press.

Huntington, John. 1989. *The Emptiness of Emptiness: an Introduction to Early Indian Mādhyamika*. Honolulu: University of Hawaii Press.

Jamgon Kongtrul. 2003. *The Autobiography of Jamgon Kongtrul*. Trans. by Richard Barron. Boston: Snow Lion Publications.

Jampa Thaye. 1990. *Garland of Gold: The Early Kagyu Masters in India and Tibet*. London: Ganesha.

— 2006. *Rain of Clarity: The Stages of the Path in the Sakya Tradition*. London: Ganesha.

Jinpa, Thubten. 2006. *Mind Training: The Great Collection*. Boston: Wisdom Publications.

— 2008. *The Book of Kadam: The Core Texts*. Boston: Wisdom Publications.

— 2013. *Wisdom of the Kadam Masters*. Boston: Wisdom Publications.

Kassor, Constance. 2011. 'Gorampa Sonam Senge on the Refutation of the Four Extremes'. *Revue d'études tibétaines* 22: 121–37.

Keown, Damien. 2005. *Buddhist Ethics: A Very Short Introduction*. Oxford: Oxford University Press.

Linrothe, Robert. 2004. *Paradise and Plumage: Chinese Connections in Tibetan Arhat Painting*. New York: Serindia.

Macintyre, Alastair. 2011 [1981]. *After Virtue: A Study in Moral Theory*. London: Bloomsbury.

Osto, Douglas. 2010. 'A New Translation of the Sanskrit *Bhadracarī* with Introduction and Notes'. *New Zealand Journal of Asian Studies* 12.2: 1–21.

Pasang Wangu and Hildegard Diemberger. 2000. *dBa' bzhed: The Royal Narrative Concerning the Bringing of the Buddha's Doctrine to Tibet*. Vienna: Verlag der Osterreichischen Akademie der Wissenschaften.

Patrul Rinpoche. 1998. *Words of My Perfect Teacher*. Trans. by Padmakara Translation Group. London: Altamira Press.

Petit, John. 2002. *Mipham's Beacon of Certainty: Illuminating the View of Dzogchen, the Great Perfection*. Boston: Wisdom Publications.

Rhys Davids, T. W. 1890. *The Questions of King Milinda*. Oxford: Clarendon Press.

van Schaik, Sam. 2004a. 'The Early Days of the Great Perfection'. *Journal of the International Association of Buddhist Studies* 27/1 (2004): 165–206.

— 2004b. *Approaching the Great Perfection: Simultaneous and Gradual Approaches to Dzogchen Practice in the Longchen Nyingtig*. Boston: Wisdom Publications.

— 2010. 'The Limits of Transgression: The Samaya Vows of Mahāyoga'. In Matthew Kapstein and Sam van Schaik (eds), *Esoteric Buddhism at Dunhuang: Rites and Teachings for this Life and Beyond*. Leiden: E. J. Brill. 61–83.

— 2011. *Tibet: A History*. London: Yale University Press.

— 2015. *Tibetan Zen: Discovering a Lost Tradition*. Boston: Shambhala.

van Schaik, Sam, and Imre Galambos. 2012. *Manuscripts and Travellers: The Sino-Tibetan Documents of a Tenth-Century Buddhist Pilgrim*. Berlin: de Gruyter.

Sherburne, Richard. 2003. *The Complete Works of Atīśa*. 2nd ed. New Delhi: Aditya Prakashan.

Skilton, Andrew. 2004. *A Concise History of Buddhism*. Birmingham: Windhorse Publications.

Sørensen, Per. 1994. *Tibetan Buddhist Historiography: The Mirror Illuminating the Royal Genealogies*. Wiesbaden: Harrossowitz Verlag.

Stearns, Cyrus. 1999. *The Buddha from Dolpo: A Study of the Life and Thought of the Tibetan Master Dolpopa Sherab Gyaltsen*. New York: State University of New York Press.

— 2001. *Luminous Lives: The Story of the Early Masters of the Lam 'Bras Tradition in Tibet*. Boston: Wisdom Publications.

Sweet, Matthew. 1996. 'Mental Purification (*Blo sbyong*): A Native Tibetan Genre of Religious Literature'. *Tibetan Literature: Studies in Genre*. Boston: Snow Lion. 244–60.

Thakchoe, Sonam. 2007. *The Two Truths Debate: Tsongkhapa and Gorampa on the Middle Way*. Boston: Wisdom Publications.

Thurman, Robert. 2009. *Life and Teachings of Tsongkhapa*. Dharamsala: Library of Tibetan Works and Archives.

Tsering, Tashi. 1985. 'Nag-roṅ Mgon-po Rnam-rgyal: A 19th Century Khams-pa Warrior'. In B. Aziz and M. Kapstein (eds), *Soundings in Tibetan Civilization*. New Delhi: Manohar. 196–214.

Tulku Thondup. 2005. *The Hidden Teachings of Tibet: An Explanation of the Terma Tradition*. 2nd ed. Boston: Wisdom Publications.

de Visser, M. V. 1923. *The Arhats in China and Japan*. Berlin: Oesterheld & Co.

Vitali, Roberto. 1996. *The Kingdoms of Gu.ge Pu.hrang*. Dharamsala: Tho.ling gtsug. lag.khang lo.gcig.stong 'khor.ba'i rjes.dran.mdzad sgo'i go.sgrig tshogs.chung.

Wallace, Vesna (ed.). 2015. *Buddhism in Mongolian History, Culture, and Society*. New York: Oxford University Press.

Williams, Paul. 2008. *Mahayana Buddhism: The Doctrinal Foundations*. 2nd ed. London: Routledge.

— 2009. 'Is Buddhist Ethics Virtue Ethics? Toward a Dialogue with Śāntideva and a Footnote to Keown'. In *Destroying Mara Forever: Buddhist Ethics. Essays in Honour of Damien Keown*. Ithaca: Snow Lion Publications. 113–37.

Tibetan Texts

Chapter 1

Letter by Patrul Rinpoche (untitled), from vol.6, 104–7 of *Collected Works*, Tib. *Gsung 'bum*. Derge: Sde dge par khang, 1970–1. W21857.

Chapter 2

A Teaching on the Ten Virtues. Tib. *Dge ba bcu'i bshad pa*, anon. In five manuscripts: IOL Tib J 606, IOL Tib J 660, Pelliot tibétain 4, Pelliot tibétain 968, Pelliot tibétain 971.

Chapter 3

Texts by Atiśa (untitled), 7–14 in *Sayings of the Kadam Masters*. Tib. *Bka' gdams kyi skyes bu dam pa rnams kyi gsung bgros thor bu ba rnams*. New Delhi: Geshe Palden Drakpa, 1983. W23746.

Chapter 4

A Key to the Profound Essential Points: A Guidance Manual on the Mind Training of Parting from the Four Attachments by Gorampa Sonam Senge. Tib. *Blo sbyong zhen pa bzhi bral gyi khrid yig zab don gnad kyi lde'u mig*. 8: 461–74 in *Collected Works*. *Gsung 'bum*. Dehradun: Sakya College, 1979. W11249.

Chapter 5

Distinguishing the Views: Moonlight upon the Essential Points of the Supreme Vehicle by Gorampa Sonam Senge. Tib. *Lta ba'i shan 'byed theg mchog gnad kyi zla zer*. 5: 417–510 in *Collected Works*. *Gsung 'bum*. Dehradun: Sakya College, 1979. W11249.

Chapter 6

Introduction to the Tantras by Sonam Tsemo. Tib. *Rgyud sde spyi'i rnam par gzhag pa*. 3: 9–156 in *The Sakya Collection*. *Sa skya bka' 'bum*. Dehradun: Sakya Centre, 1992–3. W22271.

Chapter 7

A Brief Liturgy for the Worship of the Sixteen Elders by Śākyaśrībhadra and Jamyang Khyentse Wangpo. Tib. *Gnas brtan phyag mchod dang 'brel bar cho ga mdor bsdus bya tshul*. 1: 335–44 in *Extensive Scriptures of the Early Translations*. *Snga 'gyur bka' ma shin tu rgyas pa*. Chengdu, Si khron mi rigs dpe skrun khang, 2009. WIPD100944.

Chapter 8

The Essential Biography of Jamyang Khyentse Wangpo by Jamyang Khyentse Wangpo. Tib. *'Jam dbyangs mkhyen brtse'i dbang po'i rnam thar snying por dril ba*. 22: 268–77 in *Collected Works*. *Gsung 'bum*. Gangtok: Gonpo Tseten, 1977–80. W21807.

INDEX

abhidharma, the philosophical writings included as the third part of the **tripiṭaka** 5, 69–71, 78, 113, 162

accomplishment (Skt. *siddhi*), the results of **vajrayāna** practice; 'ordinary accomplishments', such as health, wealth and intelligence, are aids on the path to enlightenment, while the 'supreme accomplishment' is enlightenment itself 101, 114, 133, 166–7, 170

afflictions (Skt. *kleśa*), negative mental states that obstruct enlightenment, including the three or five **poisons**; *see also* **obscurations** 84, 92–3, 117–18, 121, 123, 130, 132

aggregates (Skt. *skandha*), the five psycho-physical constituents of a person: (i) form, (ii) sensation, (iii) perception, (iv) formations, and (v) **consciousness** 74, 76, 84, 89, 92–5, 121, 129

arhat, one who has attained the highest level of realization as a **hearer**; considered inferior to the state of **buddhahood** 26, 115, 136, 143–51

aspirational prayer (Tib. *smon lam*), prayers expressing the aspiration of the **bodhisattva**, to bring all **sentient beings** to **enlightenment** 136–7, 139–40, 144, 152

Avalokiteśvara, a **bodhisattva** who embodies the principle of universal **compassion** 57, 101, 104

awakening mind (Skt. *bodhicitta*), the aspiration to achieve awakening, i.e. **enlightenment**, for the sake of all **sentient beings** 43–5, 49, 51–4, 59–68, 99, 102, 125–6, 132, 141

bardo, the state experienced by **sentient beings** between death and the next rebirth 140–1

Bhagavān, an epithet of the **Buddha** 99, 112, 118

bodhisattva, I. a Buddhist practitioner who aspires to bring all beings to **enlightenment** 3, 15, 19–20, 34–6, 43, 46, 53–4, 58–9, 95, 98, 107, 118, 126, 139, 162; II. a **deity** embodying a particular enlightened quality, such as **Avalokiteśvara** 36, 48, 67, 101, 129, 136–8, 141–2, 144, 149, 152, 158–9

Bon, Tibetan school with teachings and practices drawn from both Buddhist and pre-Buddhist sources, recently accepted as one of the schools of Tibetan Buddhism 164

Buddha / buddha, I. the historical buddha **Śākyamuni** 2–3, 5–6, 15, 18–19, 32, 58, 75, 100–1, 112, 114, 135–6, 148, 154, 163; II. other enlightened teachers such as **Maitreya** 54, 57, 66–7, 100–4, 131–4, 137–8, 141–4, 151–2, 159, 168; III. any sentient being who has attained full **enlightenment** 8, 15, 35, 53, 65, 100, 107–8, 115, 136